DERBYSHIRE PARISH
CHURCHES

DERBYSHIRE PARISH
CHURCHES

From the eighth to the eighteenth centuries

John Leonard

Foreword by the Rt.Rev.Peter Dawes, Bishop of Derby

The Breedon Books
Publishing Company
Derby

First published in Great Britain by
The Breedon Books Publishing Company Limited
44 Friar Gate, Derby DE1 1DA
1993

For Nancy and Keith

All royalties from the sale of this book will be devoted to the Church
Urban Fund of the Diocese of Derby.

ISBN 1 873626 36 3

Printed and bound by Hillman Printers (Frome) Ltd.
Covers printed by BDC Printing Services Ltd of Derby.

Contents

Introduction: visiting Derbyshire churches 9
The Anglo-Saxon Church in Derbyshire 11
   St Wystan, REPTON 13
   Anglo-Saxon sculpture 15
   Danish rule and Saxon re-conquest 18
The Arrival of the Normans 19
   Norman Sculpture 20
   All Saints, STEETLEY 21
   St Michael with St Mary, MELBOURNE 24
   Transitional building 27
The Early English Style – the thirteenth century 30
   St Oswald, ASHBOURNE 30
The Decorated Style – the fourteenth century 36
   St Mary and All Saints, CHESTERFIELD 37
   St John the Baptist, TIDESWELL 39
The Perpendicular Style – 1350-1550 42
Other Medieval Churches 44
   All Saints, ASHOVER 44
   All Saints, ASTON-UPON-TRENT 46
   St John the Baptist, AULT HUCKNALL 47
   All Saints, BAKEWELL 48
   St Mary, BOLSOVER 49
   All Saints, BRADBOURNE 51
   All Saints, BRAILSFORD 52
   St James, BRASSINGTON 53
   St Edmund, CASTLETON 53
   St Michael, CHURCH BROUGHTON 54
   St Mary, CRICH 56
   St Andrew, CUBLEY 57
   All Saints, DALE ABBEY 57
   St John the Baptist, DETHICK 58
   St Peter and St Paul, ECKINGTON 59
   St Lawrence, EYAM 61
   St Edmund, FENNY BENTLEY 62
   St Giles, GREAT LONGSTONE 64
   St Giles, HARTINGTON 65
   St Michael, HATHERSAGE 67
   St Mary, ILKESTON 68
   All Saints, KEDLESTON 68
   Holy Trinity, KIRK IRETON 70
   St Michael, KIRK LANGLEY 71
   St Chad, LONGFORD 72
   St Matthew, MORLEY 74
   All Saints, MUGGINTON 76
   St Mary and St Barlok, NORBURY 77
   St Andrew, RADBURNE 79
   St Giles, SANDIACRE 80
   All Saints, SAWLEY 81
   St John the Baptist, STAVELEY 82
   St Mary, TISSINGTON 83
   St Andrew, TWYFORD 84
   St Mary, WESTON-UPON-TRENT 85
   St Lawrence, WHITWELL 87
   St Chad, WILNE 87
   All Saints, WINGERWORTH 88
   St Mary, WIRKSWORTH 89
   All Saints, YOULGREAVE 91
The Age of Religious Strife – 1550-1700 94
   St Saviour, FOREMARK 94
The Eighteenth Century 96
   St Martin, STONEY MIDDLETON 96
   All Saints, DERBY (Derby Cathedral) 97
Works of Art in Derbyshire Churches 102
   Alabaster Monuments 102
   Woodwork 102
   Sedilia and piscinae 107
   Fonts 108
   Stained glass .109
Glossary 110
Bibliography 111
Index 112

Foreword

I am delighted to commend the enclosed book by Dr Leonard. Derbyshire has an extraordinary number of fine churches, many with unusual and interesting features. Curiously, they do not always seem to get the attention they deserve and this may have something to do with counties like Derbyshire being less known to tourists than other places.

Dr Leonard's book is one of the contributions which is helping to remedy that situation. Looking at churches has long been a hobby of his, and both the text and the photographs point to an enthusiast who is also extremely knowledgeable. I hope and believe this will serve to make Derbyshire churches better known to many more people.

I am also glad to commend this book in another way because, most generously, Dr Leonard has said that any profits will go towards the Church Urban Fund; but let me make it clear that I wish to commend the book in its own right as most useful and helpful to those who are unaware of the great heritage we have in Derbyshire of fine churches.

Peter Derby

Acknowledgements

Many people have helped in the production of this book. Chiefly I must express my thanks to Mrs J.Morgan of Photoworld, Altrincham for her skill in developing all the black-and-white photographs. I am also most grateful to the many incumbents of the various churches, who have lent me their keys at unseasonable times, answered my questions, and generously given of their time and knowledge. The Reverend John Drackley has very kindly read the text and saved me from error in various places; I of course am responsible for any mistakes that remain, and also for the opinions expressed. Finally I must thank my wife and sons for their oft-tested patience and endurance in searching out old churches in various parts of the country.

(Fig 1) **St Oswald, Ashbourne** *View from the south.*

Introduction —
Visiting Derbyshire Churches

Like Van Dyck's famous portrait of Charles I, Derbyshire presents three faces to the onlooker: the tourist country of high moorland and lovely dales, in the Peak District National Park; the pastoral area of countryside stretching west from Derby to the Staffordshire border; and industrial Derbyshire from Chesterfield south along the border with Nottinghamshire to Derby itself. Mention Derbyshire to an outsider, and the Peak immediately comes to mind; yet to those who live within the county the other areas are probably regarded as more typical.

Visitors come here for the scenery, the stately homes, the well-dressings — but probably not for the churches. And yet who, driving through Ashbourne, has not been struck at the majesty of the church there (Fig.1)? Or travelling from Chapel-en-le-Frith to Chesterfield, who can see the tower of Tideswell peeping over the surrounding moorland without realising that a church of mighty proportions lies beneath it? But for every hundred people who have noticed the churches at Ashbourne and Tideswell, only a handful will actually have taken the trouble to explore them. This is a pity, for the first division of Derbyshire churches can bear comparison with the finest in the country.

What constitutes the first division is, of course, a matter of opinion; but in addition to the two mentioned above, I would add Repton, Steetley chapel, Melbourne, and Chesterfield, with Bakewell, Wirksworth and Youlgreave not far behind, and, in a category of its own, All Saints, Derby, now the cathedral. But in addition to these celebrated few, there are a large number of more or less obscure churches that are waiting to be discovered; often these may be even more rewarding to visit than the well-known ones.

I came to the churches of Derbyshire having studied in the past two years those of Cheshire and Shropshire. What a contrast there is in the churches of these three more or less neighbouring counties! In Cheshire, there are few Norman churches and nearly all the best are Perpendicular. In Shropshire, there are over

(Fig 2) **All Saints, Bakewell** *Centre of an extensive Saxon parish.*

a hundred churches of Norman origin, and relatively few of the Decorated and Perpendicular styles. In Derbyshire, we have some fine Norman, Early English and Decorated churches, but a dearth of Perpendicular. Why are there these differences between adjacent shires? The answer must lie in their different histories, their varying degrees of economic prosperity and consequent changes in population. These and other factors are explored in the pages that follow.

So I came to Derbyshire in the spring of 1991 and visited nearly all of the 150 or so churches which date before 1800. I have chosen 49 of these to illustrate the evolution of the church in Derbyshire, from the eighth to the eighteenth centuries; the great majority are set in attractive surroundings, and they have been selected in the hope that readers of this book may be tempted to explore the wonders of these buildings so rich in architecture, history and art, some of them of national importance. In describing them, I have used the traditional classification of medieval churches into Norman, Early English, Decorated and Perpendicular, but perhaps a note of warning is necessary for the uninitiated. These named periods of building are the result of retrospective analysis of building styles; they did not, of course, exist in the minds of the builders. In response to changing fashion, one style merged imperceptibly into the next, usually as a result of new trends imported from the continent. And because people moved very little in the Middle Ages, it might, and often did, take fifty years for a style to spread from London and the southeast to distant counties in the north and west. So dates of specific buildings must be interpreted cautiously, for there is rarely documentary evidence of a precise date of construction.

The pleasure of visiting ancient churches is

(Fig 3) **All Saints, Aston-upon-Trent** *Saxon long-and-short work.*

not of course confined to those who have a primarily religious interest. The history, architecture, art and craftsmanship displayed have a much broader appeal. But to those who believe, there is an added dimension of wonder and joy that the faith to which these churches bear witness is so beautifully expressed in wood and stone.

The Anglo-Saxon Church In Derbyshire

Following the departure of the Roman legions from Britain in AD410, the country became subject to recurring invasions of Germanic peoples — the Angles, Saxons and Jutes — who displaced the native British to the north and west. By the seventh century, the newcomers had coalesced into seven kingdoms (the *Heptarchy*): the Angles in Northumberland and East Anglia; the Jutes in Kent; the Saxons in Essex, Sussex and Wessex; and last to emerge, the central Kingdom of Mercia, of which Derbyshire was a part. The Anglo-Saxons probably first penetrated into Derbyshire in the early seventh century and Repton became their chief settlement (Childs).

Mercia was the last of the seven kingdoms formally to adopt Christianity. At the end of the sixth century (597), Pope Gregory had sent St Augustine to Kent, whence the faith gradually spread through neighbouring areas. In the north and west, pockets of Christianity persisted from Roman times, especially in those areas where the faith could be nourished by contacts with the Celtic church in Ireland. But Mercia remained obdurately pagan, and for many years in the mid-seventh century it was ruled by the fierce heathen King Penda. He killed the Christian King Oswald of Northumbria in 642 and met his end at the hands of Oswald's brother Oswy in 655. Two years later Penda's son and heir Peada was baptised, and he married into the Christian Northumbrian royal family; the formal conversion of Mercia rapidly followed. Four missionary priests were sent from Northumbria to evangelise the pagan kingdom: Chad (Ceadda), Adda, Betti and Diuma. Chad, the first bishop of Mercia, was appointed in 669 by Peada's successor, Wulfhere, and fixed his see at Lichfield.

It seems that Repton was the capital of Mercia at that time, and it was therefore natural that the first Christian foundation in Derbyshire was established here, apparently by Diuma *c*.660. From then until 874 it was the leading religious establishment in the region. Although it was a Benedictine abbey for both monks and nuns, it was ruled by an abbess.

For the next hundred years, Mercia became steadily more powerful, and under two successive kings in the eighth century (Aethelbald and Offa) it became the dominant power in the land. Aethelbald was murdered in 757 at Seckington, and was buried at Repton; it seems likely that the surviving crypt at Repton was first built as his mausoleum. The leading scholar of Repton, Dr H.M.Taylor, believes that the vaulting of the crypt and the building of the chancel above were the work of the later Mercian King Wiglaf, who died in 840 and was buried there. His grandson, Wystan, was murdered in 849 and was also buried there. He was later canonised, and his shrine became a place of pilgrimage. The present parish church is dedicated to him.

But the days of Repton's glory were now approaching their end. The power of Mercia had waned in the ninth century as Wessex finally emerged as the greatest kingdom of Anglo-Saxon times. Disaster struck in 874 when the invading Danes spent the winter in Repton and destroyed the abbey. They had begun to harry the east coast in 787, and in the ninth century steadily extended their raids, beginning to penetrate inland and to settle for the winter in various parts of eastern England. After the sack of Repton, the Danes became the dominant power in Derbyshire.

During the Anglo-Saxon centuries, it is now apparent that many more churches were founded than previously believed. Those that have survived are only a miniscule proportion of the total. The churches were nearly all built of wood, and so have perished without trace. Stone was used only for cathedrals and monasteries until *c*.950, but thereafter was used increasingly for some parish churches. But it was not until a hundred years later that large-scale stone building for local churches was undertaken.

The organisation of the church in Saxon times was relatively loose. Originally, a number of minsters arose, usually serving a very wide area (eg Bakewell Fig.2), and being staffed by a variable number of canons. In the later Saxon centuries, many village churches were founded by laymen, with only a tenuous relationship with the local bishop. These churches were often regarded by the local thane as part of his personal property, almost as a capital investment; for ownership of a church increasingly brought in revenue in the form of tithes. So the large areas originally served by the older minsters became progressively smaller as parishes multiplied.

There are a number of characteristic features which identify Saxon stonework. At corners, slabs were often set alternately vertically and

(Fig 4) **St Wystan, Repton** *Fourteenth-century tower and recessed spire.*

horizontally — long-and-short work (Fig.3) — a feature not found in Norman building. Saxon masonry of this type may be seen at Repton and Aston-upon-Trent. Herringbone masonry (though not confined to Saxon building) consists of rows of stones applied diagonally, each row leaning alternately to the right and the left. For decoration, very typical Saxon features are tall thin strips or pilasters - thin flat stones applied vertically — well seen on the outer walls of the chancel at Repton (Fig.5). Saxon doorways are plain. Saxon windows are small, usually high up, and sometimes splayed equally both inside and outside (Norman windows are splayed internally). They may be round-headed or triangular-headed; a possible example of the former is the window above the tower arch in the west wall at Mugginton (Fig. 127, p.76).

The only church in Derbyshire with significant Saxon work is St Wystan's, Repton, so our survey of Derbyshire parish churches must begin there. Several other churches (Aston-upon-Trent, Bradbourne, Stanton-by-Bridge) show some evidence of Saxon workmanship, but have nothing comparable with the glory of Repton.

St Wystan, Repton

The building history of St Wystan's is by far the most complex in the county, and has been studied with great care by Dr H.M.Taylor during the past fifty years. His excellent and scholarly guide is available in the church, and I have relied greatly on it in the description that follows.

In order to appreciate the church's history, it is perhaps best to study the exterior before going inside the building. As one approaches from the south, the eye is first arrested by the splendid fourteenth century tower, surmounted by battlements and corner pinnacles and a spire which attains a height of 212 feet (Fig.4). Notice the thirteenth century Early English lancet window at the west end of the south aisle, just to the left of the porch. The porch itself, and the clerestory above the nave are fifteenth-century Perpendicular. The aisles, north and south, were widened early in the fourteenth century, and their windows, and that at the east end of the chancel, show intersecting tracery of the Decorated period.

Go next to the east end of the nave, the chancel and the crypt below, for here is evidence of Saxon work of the greatest importance. The lowest part of the masonry is a brownish stone, and above this the stonework is whiter, with a horizontal string-course (Fig.5). This string-course goes all around the chancel and the

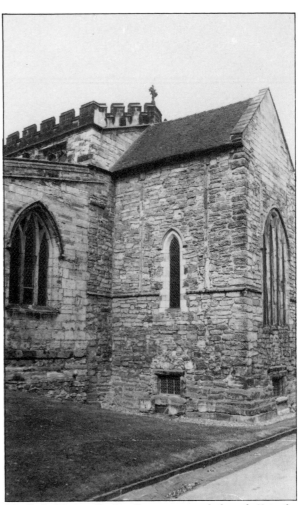

(Fig 5) **St Wystan, Repton** *Saxon crypt and chancel. Note the vertical pilasters and horizontal string-course. The vertical demarcation between the Saxon and medieval masonry is clearly shown, and the difference between the earlier darker Saxon masonry and the later Saxon masonry is also apparent.*

adjacent part of the nave, being interrupted only by the insertion into the Saxon walls of the east window in the fourteenth century, and of the lancet windows in the north and south walls of the chancel; the lancet in the north wall dates from the thirteenth century, but the south lancet was inserted only in 1940. From the string-course ascend narrow vertical pilaster strips, typical of Saxon workmanship. Notice the windows of the crypt, and, on the south side, two large projecting stones resting on the sill which may have supported a gabled projection. At the east end of the south aisle, to the left of the chancel, there is an obvious vertical line which demarcates the Saxon building from the widening of the aisles in the fourteenth century. Dr Taylor believes that the earliest phase in the building of the crypt and chancel is defined by the brownish masonry which extends to about two feet below the string-course, and that this part was built as a mausoleum, possibly for King Aethelbald, in the eighth century. The whiter masonry above he attributes to the building of King Wiglaf, *c*.830-839.

Internally, the north and south arcades (Fig.6) were built in the fourteenth century, except for

(Fig 6) **St Wystan, Repton** *The south arcade, and Saxon masonry above the chancel arch.*

the two eastern arches which date from 1854 and replaced the original Anglo-Saxon work; the wall above these two arches is still, however, part of the original masonry. As already noted, the clerestory is Perpendicular, as is the fine panelled low-pitched roof (Fig.7). Evidence of the earlier steeply-pitched roof can be seen above the tower arch at the west end of the nave. At the east end of the nave, the chancel arch dates from the fourteenth century, having been inserted into the Anglo-Saxon masonry. Notice the contrast between the rough stones of the Saxon building above the chancel arch and the eastern two arches of the nave compared with the smoother walling of the fourteenth century above the western four arches. Above the chancel arch can be seen a modern doorway (Fig.6); to the right of this, the stones are laid in a typical Anglo-Saxon manner, being alternately set upright and flat (long-and-short work). The discerning may also be able to make out that eight feet to the north (left) there is a similar jamb set in an apparently undisturbed part of the wall. It is thought that these two jambs originally defined a wide doorway opening into a chamber above the chancel. Inside the chancel itself may be seen marks high up on the side walls of beams which could have carried the floor of this chamber.

The crypt (Fig.8), of course, is the *pièce-de-résistance*, one of the greatest architectural

treasures of Anglo-Saxon England. Stairs lead down from the north chapel into the northwest corner of the crypt. The lower stairs are very worn and irregular due to the tread of innumerable pilgrims to the shrine of St Wystan from the time of his death in 849 to the removal of his remains to Evesham early in the eleventh century. The crypt has a vaulted ceiling of nine bays supported on round arches springing from square pilasters beside the wall, and resting on four central columns. Each column is decorated with two spiral fillets ascending from base to capital. From the central square chamber four rectangular recesses lead outward; these are contained in the thickness of the original walls without any outward projection.

The successive stages in the building of St Wystan's may therefore be summarised as follows (adapted from Taylor):

1. In the early eighth century, the lower part of the crypt in brownish stone, of which about two metres were below ground and one metre above.

2. During Wiglaf's reign (827-839), the chancel was built above the crypt, using whiter stone, and also the eastern part of the present nave.

3. Between 849 and 873. Some time after the death of Wystan (849) and before the Danish assault (874), stairs were cut from the western

(Fig 8) **St Wystan, Repton** *Interior of the crypt.*

(Fig 7) **St Wystan, Repton** *The Perpendicular roof.*

corners of the crypt to cater for the pilgrims visiting the shrine.

4. Thirteenth century (Early English). The south aisle was widened to its present dimensions (see the lancet window at the west end of the south aisle).

5. Fourteenth century (Decorated). Widening of the north aisle to its present alignment; the four western arches of the nave; windows in the aisles and the east window in the chancel.

6. Fifteenth century (Perpendicular). The tower and clerestory, and the roof over the nave. *Access:* From Derby, take the A38 in a southwesterly direction towards Burton-on-Trent. After about six miles, follow a left turning (B5008) through Willington to Repton. St Wystan's is on the left as you enter the town.

Anglo-Saxon Sculpture

In addition to the work at Repton, there are in Derbyshire a remarkable series of Saxon crosses; even more impressive is the Wirksworth stone, the greatest treasure in any Derbyshire church.

Modern county boundaries have, of course, little significance for Anglo-Saxon times, so when considering Anglo-Saxon sculpture in present-day Derbyshire it is wholly artificial to

(Fig 9) **All Saints, Bradbourne** *Saxon cross showing the Crucifixion.*

(Fig 10) **St Lawrence, Eyam** *Saxon cross. Vine-scroll on the shaft, and angels on the arms of the cross.*

ignore the leading school of Mercian sculpture which arose in the eighth century at Breedon-on-the-Hill, which is now just inside Leicestershire, though only two miles from Melbourne and eight from Repton. Here, *c*.675, a Benedictine Abbey was founded by the Mercian king Aethelred, and like Repton it was sacked by the Danes in 874. The astonishing works produced here may still be seen in the parish church of St Mary. Pevsner writes as follows: 'The sculpture is mostly in the form of friezes. They . . .contain geometrical ornament, Greek keys, pelta forms etc., interlace, and in addition vine or ivy scrolls, not as tight and springy as those of the eighth-century crosses of the North, animals and birds, not realistically but fantastically treated, big-bellied beasts, and crane-necked birds, and also human figures, including some on horseback with spears, and others kneeling and seated'.

The vine-scroll is a Christian motif arising in the Near East and Mediterranean (Wilson), probably ultimately deriving from the fifteenth chapter of St John's Gospel ('I am the true vine'). In Anglo-Saxon sculpture it may often be difficult to recognise as a vine, and the term 'plant-scroll' is sometimes used instead. Fronded leaves and bunches of grapes may be

seen, and somtimes the motif takes the form of a tree (the Tree of Life). Frequently the plant-scrolls may be 'inhabited', featuring birds, animals, monsters and sometimes human figures. Fret and interlace patterns similar to those found in early Northumbrian manuscripts may also be seen.

Breedon flourished during the era of Mercian supremacy, that is during and shortly after the reigns of Aethelbald (726-757) and Offa (757-796). The Derbyshire sculpture which derives from the school comprises the standing crosses at Bakewell, Bradbourne and Eyam, and the fragmentary cross-shaft at St Alkmund's, Derby, now in the Derby Museum and Art Gallery. At Bakewell there are vine-scrolls and animals, and on the west side a series of sculptures of human figures, the upper one being the Crucifixion. The cross is eight feet high, excluding the base. At Bradbourne (Fig.9), the shaft again depicts the Crucifixion and other faces show vine-scroll decoration. At Eyam (Fig.10), the cross is remarkable for the survival of the cross-head on the arms of which are carved angels blowing musical instruments. On the shaft are coarse vine-scrolls and interlace pattern.

The cross-shaft from St Alkmund's is

(Fig 11) **All Saints, Brailsford** *Saxon cross showing interlace and a human figure.*

probably later, ninth century rather than eighth, because it is thought to show evidence of Scandinavian influence. The area around Derby was settled by the Danes in the last quarter of the ninth century, after the sacking of Repton and Breedon, and the sculpture from St Alkmund's is said to show a synthesis of Anglo-Saxon and Scandinavian styles (Wilson).

From late in the Anglo-Saxon period, in the eleventh century, a larger group of crosses survive, including those at Blackwell, Brailsford (Fig.11), Darley Dale, Hope, Norbury, Taddington, and Two Dales (now in the porch at Bakewell). Across the county border into Staffordshire, similar crosses may be seen at Ilam, Leek and Checkley. Most of these crosses show prominent interlace patterns, sometimes with human figures also, and are thought to show close affinities with contemporary Anglo-Danish work in Cumberland (eg Gosforth, Beckermet St John).

The Wirksworth Stone
The stone in the north wall of St Mary's, Wirksworth (Fig.12) was unearthed in 1820 when the pavement in front of the altar was removed. The dating of Anglo-Saxon sculpture is full of hazard, but most authorities seem to regard it as *c*.800. It is regarded as one of the most outstanding pieces of Anglo-Saxon sculputre extant. The following is largely taken

(Fig 12) **St Mary, Wirksworth** *Saxon tombstone.*

from the description by R.W.P.Cockerton from the Archaeological Journal of 1961.

When found, the stone was two feet below the surface with the carving downward and it covered a stone-built vault or grave containing a large perfect human skeleton. The stone shows affinities with Eastern or Byzantine iconography rather than Latin or Western use, the scenes having parallels with those connected with the Eastern festival cycles.

In the upper tier, the scenes from left to right are: (1) Christ washing the disciples' feet (other authorities describe this as St Mary Magdalene washing the feet of Christ); (2) The Crucifixion, with the lamb slain on a Grecian type cross; this symbol of the lamb slain upon the cross was banned by the Council of Constantinople of 692; (3) the body of the Virgin Mary being borne out for burial, headed by St John bearing a palm, other apostles carrying the body of the Virgin on a stretcher and the High Priest who seized hold of the bier being dragged beneath; this scene is derived from the Apocryphal New Testament and is thought to be the earliest known portrayal in Western art, enshrining the idea of the Assumption of the Blessed Virgin; (4) the presentation of Christ in the temple, with St Simeon holding the baby in his arms (Luke ii. 25-35).

In the lower tier are (1) the Descent into hell; (2) the Ascension; (3) the Annunciation; and (4) the scene on the right apparently portraying St Peter standing in a boat (representing the Church) indicating how the Word of God is to be transmitted to the Gentiles.

Danish Rule and Saxon Re-conquest

Following the sack of the Mercian capital in 874, Alfred the Great, King of Wessex, bought peace with the Danes with money known as the Danegeld. Four years later he defeated them in battle, and negotiated a treaty restricting the Danes to the area east of Watling Street, running from the West Midlands to London. The Danish region was known as the Danelaw, and Derbyshire lay within it, but on its western frontier. The Danes had a lasting influence on the county, and the area governed from Derby ultimately became the present county. The Danes subdivided the shire not into Saxon hundreds but into 'wapentakes' (though later they were commonly called hundreds), which remained in existence for eight hundred years. The frequency of Danish placenames, especially those ending in -*by*, testifies to their lasting influence.

Alfred's settlement with the Danes divided Mercia into two, and the situation was highly unstable. During his reign, the remnant of Mercia became virtually a dependency of Wessex (Ethelred, King of Mercia, married Alfred's daughter Aethelflaed, known as the Lady of the Mercians.) By 917 her troops had recaptured Derby and two years later her brother Edward (Alfred's son and successor) reconquered the Peak. He formally annexed Mercia to the kingdom of Wessex by being proclaimed king of the Anglo-Saxons. Derby was briefly again subdued by the Danes before being recaptured by King Athelstan in 937.

During these troubled times, some of the Danes embraced Christianity and Derby itself had six parishes by the time of the Norman conquest. Anglo-Saxon and Danish influence clearly continued side by side: two of the dedications of Derby churches were to St Alkmund and St Werburgh. These two saints were of Anglo-Saxon origin, St Alkmund being the younger son of Alhred, King of Northumbria, and St Werburgh being the niece of King Ethelred of Mercia.

During the reign of Athelstan (King of All Britain), Derby was an important centre, and the site of a royal mint. His successors more or less kept the Danes at bay until the disastrous reign of Ethelred (the Unready; 978-1916); this was followed by Danish rule over the entire country by King Canute (1016-1035). The Anglo-Saxon line was restored in the person of Edward the Confessor in 1042, and his death in 1066 opened the way to King Harold, the Battle of Hastings, and the triumph of William the Conqueror.

The Arrival of the Normans

The victory of William the Conqueror over King Harold at the Battle of Hastings in 1066 ended Anglo-Saxon England for ever; ended also after a short time were the incessant conflicts with the Danes. But peace was bought at the price of subjugation of the people to an alien, oppressive rule; and the peasantry witnessed the appropriation of all the most valuable assets by the Norman invaders. In the north especially there was seething discontent which erupted in open rebellion in 1069-70. William's response, after crushing the uprising, was the *harrying of the north* — systematic pillage and despoliation of the countryside, which laid waste to vast tracts of land.

Twenty years after the Battle of Hastings, the Domesday survey was made, and reveals that Derbyshire was still bearing the scars of William's iron rule. 43 settlements were still described as waste, and another 25 were partly waste. The king had taken for himself large parts of the county, the chief lay magnate being Henry de Ferrers whose son became the first Earl of Derby.

The Normans brought with them their own style of Romanesque architecture, and in the twelfth century a comprehensive programme of church building was begun. In Derbyshire, as elsewhere, there must have been innumerable Saxon churches constructed of wood, and these of course have not survived. They were now replaced by buildings of stone on an extensive scale.

In the smallest Norman churches, there was just a nave and chancel, and this is to be seen in its purest form in Steetley chapel. The outstanding example in Derbyshire of Norman building on a substantial scale is the church of St Michael with St Mary at Melbourne. Many Norman churches began on a small scale and then had to be enlarged to cater for the expanding population which occurred in the twelfth and thirteenth centuries. This was done by lateral extension of the nave in the form of aisles, separated from the nave by arcades of semicircular arches supported by massive cylindrical piers or columns (Fig.13). The piers are surmounted by square-edged capitals (Fig.14) which effect the transition from the round column to the square abacus above which supports the arch. The inferior surface of the capital is often carved into a cushion (a rounding-off of the lower angles into the cylindrical shaft below), scallop (a further modification in which the surface is elaborated

(Fig 13) **All Saints, Youlgreave** *Norman arcade.*

19

(Fig 14) **All Saints, Youlgreave** *Norman capital decorated with volutes and heads.*

into a series of truncated cones) or volute (spiral scrolls).

Semicircular arches are also found above doorways and windows, and are, of course, the hallmark of Norman architecture. They often became decorated by geometric designs, the commonest being the chevron or zigzag (Figs.15 and 16), which was introduced *c*.1120. Other Norman ornamental motifs are beakhead (the repeated use of stylised heads of birds or mammals with long beaks — see Fig.80, p.51), billet (short raised rectangles placed at regular intervals) and nail-head (small pyramids regularly repeated). Late in the Norman period, and continuing more typically into the next century, dog-tooth occurs (a series of four-cornered stars placed diagonally and raised pyramidally). Norman windows (Figs.17 and 27) are usually small and round-headed, and are deeply splayed internally (but not externally) to maximise the provison of light, glass being expensive.

Norman towers are squat, sturdy, plain, solidly-built, with thick walls (Fig.18). At belfry level, there are usually two round-headed windows divided by a shaft, with a larger round-headed arch surmounting both.

In addition to parish churches, a number of monasteries were founded, but little has survived. The main ones were: Darley (one mile north of Derby), an Augustinian abbey founded *c*.1146 by Robert Ferrers, Earl of Derby; Repton, re-founded after destruction by the Danes in 1172 as an Augustinian priory; Dale, founded

(Fig 15) **St Peter, Parwich** *Norman doorway with chevron decoration above.*

as an Augustinian priory *c*.1155, and re-founded as a Premonstratensian abbey *c*.1198; and Breadsall Priory, founded in the first half of the thirteenth century.

Steetley and Melbourne are the finest examples of Norman building in Derbyshire because they have been left relatively untouched in succeeding ages, and therefore they retain a purity of Norman style not seen elsewhere.

Norman Sculpture

Above a Norman doorway was usually placed a horizontal stone, or lintel, and the space above this and below the rounded arch is known as the tympanum. In late Saxon times, but more especially in the Norman twelfth century, tympana were often given special treatment by the stonemasons, being carved with various motifs, some simple and geometrical, others representational, a few exquisite. They were first systematically studied and described by C.E.Keyser in 1904, and he listed fifteen in Derbyshire, more than in any other county except Gloucestershire (22) and Oxfordshire (16).

(Fig 16) **St Michael, Alsop-en-le-Dale** *A double zigzag pattern above the Norman doorway.*

The Derbyshire tympana are best described as quaint and interesting, rather than beautiful; certainly there is nothing in the county to compare with the marvellous example at Aston Eyre in Shropshire. Geometrical patterns of stars, crosses and circles can be seen at Scarcliffe, Tissington (Fig.19) and Findern, the last two having human figures at each side. Scenes comprising strange beasts are found at Ashford-in-the-Water, Hognaston and Parwich. The interpretation of these three is obscure: at Ashford (Fig.20) there is a hog and another animal on either side of the Tree of Life; at Hognaston (Fig.21), a hog and other creatures accompany a bishop, apparently to worship the Agnus Dei (the Lamb of God); at Parwich (Fig.22), the lamb supporting a wheel-cross is confronted by various creatures including a stag, a bird, a pig and a lion. At Bolsover, the rather worn carving is of a Crucifixion (Fig.23) flanked by the Virgin Mary and St John. At Ault Hucknall, perhaps the best preserved, the tympanum depicts the legend of St Margaret of Antioch (Fig.24); she is shown as emerging from the body of the evil one who had swallowed her through the power of the Cross depicted as the Lamb of God bearing a cross. Below on the lintel are carved figures of St George and the dragon, separated by a large cross (Keyser).

Norman sculpture may also be studied in a number of fonts in the county. Those at Eyam (Fig.25) and Hognaston (Fig.26) both show plain arcaded patterns. Other notable Norman fonts are at Chesterfield, Church Broughton, Tissington and Youlgreave. The remarkable font at Ashover is the finest of all, being made of lead (Fig.66, p.45).

All Saints, Steetley

Steetley chapel, in the extreme northeast corner of Derbyshire, stands almost alone, with just a neighbouring farm for company. There is no village of Steetley, and apparently there never has been one, for the building was erected as a chapel in the parish of Whitwell — and after a period of independence in the fourteenth century, it again became subject to Whitwell, as it is today. It become neglected early in the eighteenth century, and later was used as a barn. The British Archaeological Association visited it in 1873, when it was ruinous, without a roof and being used as a poultry yard. Fortunately a careful restoration took place a few years later, with the result that the glories of its Norman architecture have been preserved. After this, the building was 'reconciled' by the Bishop of Lichfield, and it remains in use for regular worship to this day.

The chapel is tiny, consisting only of a nave, chancel and apse with a rounded east end (Fig.27), very uncommon in Norman churches

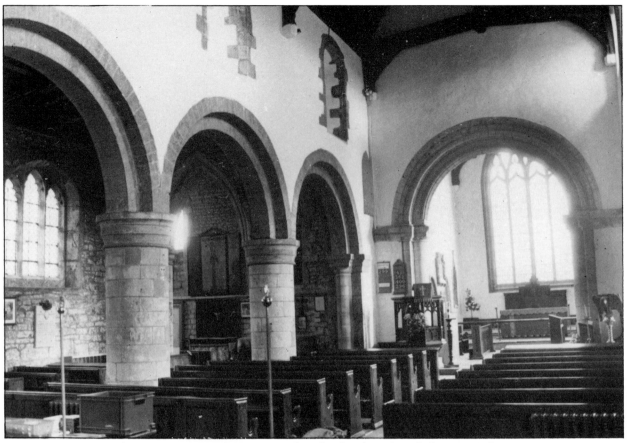

(Fig 17) **St Lawrence, Whitwell** *Norman chancel arch and arcade, with clerestory windows.*

(Fig 18) **St Leonard, Thorpe** *The Norman tower.*

(Fig 19) **St Mary, Tissington** *Norman tympanum.*

(Fig 23) **St Mary, Bolsover** *Norman tympanum.*

(Fig 20) **Holy Trinity, Ashford-in-the-Water** *Norman tympanum.*

(Fig 24) **St John the Baptist, Ault Hucknall** *Norman tympanum.*

(Fig 21) **St Bartholomew, Hognaston** *Norman tympanum.*

(Fig 22) **St Peter, Parwich** *Norman tympanum.*

(Fig 25) **St Lawrence, Eyam** *Norman font.*

(Fig 26) **St Bartholomew, Hognaston** *Norman font.*

(Fig 28) **All Saints, Steetley** *The south doorway.*

(Fig 29) **All Saints, Steetley** *The chancel arch, the arch into the apse, and the vaulted apse.*

apse is very fine, with a horizontal string-course, vertical pilasters ascending from base to the eaves, and three fine Norman windows with nook-shafts.

Internally, the chapel is impressive because of the beauty of the chancel arch through which is seen the arch into the vaulted apse beyond (Fig.29), the whole composing a picture of great richness yet also of simplicity. The chancel arch has three orders of decoration, the inner one being chevron, the intermediate embattled, and the outer described by Cox as 'an escalloped border over reticulated cones'. On the capitals are carved a double-headed lion, St George and the dragon, etc. The inner arch to the apse is also triple, but is plainer, with billet decoration only on the outer order. The roof of the apse is vaulted, supported by four ribs resting on pillars; the capitals of these pillars are carved with representations of Adam and Eve, the serpent, etc. The string course which girdles the apse below the windows is beautifully carved with foliage.

Access: From Chesterfield, take the A619 towards Worksop. One mile after passing Whitwell, the main road bends towards the right; at this point turn left into a lane, and after about 300 yards take the left fork. The church will be found on the left, opposite a farm. There is room for car parking.

St Michael with St Mary, Melbourne

It is generally acknowledged that Melbourne church is one of the finest Norman parish churches anywhere in England. The reason for this is two-fold: firstly, it is on a substantial

in England though often seen on the continent. The south doorway (Fig.28) is very elaborately carved for such a small church, with four orders of colonnettes, the arches showing chevron and beakhead decoration. As Pevsner points out, much of this doorway dates from the Victorian restoration and the gable above the doorway is entirely Victorian. There are very small Norman windows in the nave, and one Decorated window in the south wall — the only post-Norman modification until the Victorian restoration. Externally, note the grotesque heads of the Norman corbel-table under the eaves, reminiscent of those seen at Kilpeck in Herefordshire. The semicircular east end of the

(Fig 27) **All Saints, Steetley** *The rounded east end.*

(Fig 30) **St Michael with St Mary, Melbourne** *The west door.*

scale, especially considering the modest size of Melbourne; and secondly, since the Norman period the church has been left virtually unchanged, almost the sole addition of note being the Perpendicular east window. So what one sees in Melbourne is an uncommonly pure Norman building which towers over the surrounding town.

The origins of St Michael's have been the subject of some uncertainty. The church was granted in 1133 by Henry I to Adelulf (or Aethelwold), when he became the first Bishop of Carlisle. Adelulf was the king's confessor and was prior of the Augustinian house at Nostell in Yorkshire. (The Augustinian priory at Carlisle became the cathedral there in 1133.) The foundation of Carlisle Cathedral buttressed the claims of the king in the interminable disputes with the Scots, but the city was not always safe for his confessor; in fact, Carlisle reverted to Scottish rule from 1136-1157. It used to be thought that Adelulf was provided with Melbourne as a safer haven in troublous times than Carlisle, and that the church was built after Adelulf's promotion to Carlisle, but it is now believed that St Michael's was built *before* Adelulf became bishop as an appendage of the king's manor of Melbourne, possibly around 1120 (Gem).

Whatever the explanation, the happy result is that Melbourne is endowed with a truly great church. From the outside, note the great west door (Fig.30) with four orders of colonnettes

(Fig 31) **St Michael with St Mary, Melbourne** *Massive Norman piers, arcade and clerestory.*

and the corresponding arches with chevron decoration. Twin towers at the west end were originally planned but never completed. At the east end there were originally three semicircular apses at the termination of the north and south transepts and the chancel. Traces of these can still be discerned.

Inside, the massive Norman pillars supporting the arches with chevron decoration are enormously impressive (Fig.31). The capitals are square, with many scallops beneath. Above the arcades is a clerestory which on the north side exhibits a Norman arcade with triple arches opening to single round-headed windows; on the south side, this was replaced in the thirteenth century with an Early English arcade of double pointed arches and pointed windows. A passageway, or ambulatory, runs all round the nave behind the clerestory arches — a unique feature in parish churches, but often found in cathedrals. At the west end, the west door opens into a vaulted narthex of three interconnected rooms — another unique feature in an English parish church, though similar examples are known in Normandy.

Between the nave and the chancel is the crossing (Fig.32), with arches to all four sides; the capitals on the eastern arches are carved with grotesques and foliage. The three tiers of Norman arcading can be seen well by looking up into the lantern above the crossing. There is a medieval wall-painting on the north-western pillar. In the chancel, the north and south windows are Norman, with nook-shafts; as already mentioned, the east window is Perpendicular.

Access: From Derby, take the A514 south; at Swarkestone the road turns left and the causeway over the Trent is crossed. The road to Melbourne (B587) is shortly after this, on the left. The church is at the south-eastern extremity of the town, adjacent to the hall.

Transitional Building

In the last forty years of the twelfth century, the gradual introduction of the Gothic style of pointed arch may be seen; where this occurs alongside Norman features, the style is known as Transitional. The introduction of the pointed arch, which was to revolutionise church architecture, was primarily for structural reasons, such an arch being able to transmit a larger proportion of the thrust directly to the ground (Foster). It appears to have been first used at Autun Cathedral, France, around 1120-1130, but was not seen in England until about 1160. From then onwards, it was seen side by side with semicircular arches (the Transitional period) until after about 1200 semicircular arches are seen no more, and the Early English period is said to have begun.

(Fig 32) **St Michael with St Mary, Melbourne** *The nave looking east.*

(Fig 33) **All Saints, Youlgreave** *Transitional north arcade.*

Although late Norman work may be seen in Derbyshire at, for example, Crich, and Whitwell, examples of the Transitional style, with Norman piers supporting pointed arches are hard to find; perhaps the best example is the north arcade at Youlgreave (Fig.33). Contrast this with the south arcade shown in Fig.13, p.19).

(Fig 34) **St Michael, Stanton-by-Bridge** *Early English arcade and Norman chancel arch.*

(Fig 35) **St Michael, Breaston** *Early English arch with rather decayed dogtooth ornamentation.*

The Early English Style
— the thirteenth century

The Early English style covers roughly the whole of the thirteenth century, and work of this period is frequently seen in Derbyshire alongside earlier Norman architecture. The reason for this is that increasing prosperity and growing population required the progressive enlargement of many churches by the addition of aisles or the lengthening of naves and chancels. Although much Norman work was sound and has stood the test of time, some was less good and required replacement. Sometimes replacement was wholesale, and preceding Saxon or Norman buildings vanished without trace, leaving us with churches which are basically Early English, with or without significant later additions. Some of the finest churches in the county come into this category — eg Ashbourne, Bakewell, Wirksworth. In other cases, Early English work may be seen alongside earlier Saxon or Norman building (eg Repton, Morley).

(Fig 36) **St Oswald, Ashbourne** *Lancet windows in the chancel.*

In Early English churches, the semicircular arches and thick cylindrical piers of the Norman age have given way to acutely-pointed arches supported by less substantial piers (Fig.34), often with fillets (thin longitudinal bands running down the shaft). There is considerable variety in the cross-section of the piers: at first they usually remain circular, but as the century progressed, octagonal or multi-shafted piers may be seen. They are now usually surmounted by capitals with a rounded (instead of a square) upper edge, and may be characteristically decorated with 'stiff-leaf' foliage. The dog-tooth pattern (Fig.35) may also be found in Early English arcades. Instead of the deeply recessed small Norman windows, tall lancet windows with acutely pointed upper ends are seen (Fig.36), often in groups of three at the east end of the chancel. Externally, lancet windows were provided with a hood-mould of projecting masonry to throw the rainwater clear of the window. Sometimes two or more lancets were enclosed by the same hood-mould to prevent the water from puddling between them; this necessarily also enclosed a small area of blank wall at the apex below the common hood-mould. Later in the century, this area was often pierced, resulting in plate or Y-tracery above the lancet windows (Fig.37). From this germ, the later development of complex tracery seen in the next century evolved.

Early English towers have pointed lancet windows, and the belfry windows become more prominent (Fig.38). Spires were sometimes built in the thirteenth century — usually broach spires in which semipyramidal pieces of masonry at the top of the tower effected a smooth transition to the octagonal spire (Fig.39). Buttresses in the thirteenth century were usually placed at each corner, at right angles to each other. The projection of the buttresses diminishes towards the top of the tower, and was reduced stepwise with a sloping set-off to shed rainwater.

St Oswald, Ashbourne

Ashbourne parish church is one of the glories of Derbyshire: its tower and soaring spire dominate the small town (Fig.1, p.8) and the excellence of the church must be apparent to the casual passer-by.

St Oswald was a popular Anglo-Saxon saint:

(Fig 37) **All Saints, Bakewell** *Paired lancet windows under a common hood-mould; pierced spandrels with Y-tracery.*

(Fig 38) **All Saints, Breadsall** *Thirteenth-century tower with belfry windows; fourteenth-century recessed spire.*

(Fig 39) **St Peter and St Paul, Brampton** *Thirteenth-century tower and broach spire.*

(Fig 41) **St Oswald, Ashbourne** *The south arcade.*

(Fig 40) **St Oswald, Ashbourne** *The chancel with the Perpendicular east window.*

Ashbourne is the only medieval dedication to him in Derbyshire, but there are five in Cheshire, and he gave his name to Oswaldkirk (Yorkshire), Oswaldtwistle (Lancashire) and Oswestry (Shropshire). He became King of Northumbria (635-642) and brought St Aidan from Iona to Lindisfarne; their efforts were largely responsible for the conversion of that kingdom and the foundation of the Northumbrian church.

Ashbourne means 'stream where ash trees grow', and is thus the old name for Henmore Brook which flows through the town on its way to join the river Dove at Church Mayfield. The church is mentioned in Domesday Book, and it must be presumed that there was a Saxon building here, and also a later Norman one. William II gave the church to the Dean and Chapter of Lincoln Cathedral, and apart from a short hiatus in the thirteenth century, it remained in their hands until Victorian times, when it was transferred to the bishop of Lichfield.

Saxon and Norman work perished without trace, but the existence of a Norman crypt was confirmed during excavations in 1913. The present building is Early English, and can be dated to 1241 by an inscription on a small brass plate in the south transept. The earliest part of the building is the chancel, which has a lovely array of Early English lancet windows in the

(Fig 42) **St Oswald, Ashbourne** *Leaf capitals.*

north and south walls (Fig.36, p.30); internally these windows have nook-shafts. The seven-light east window is a later insertion in the Perpendicular fashion (Fig.40). The stained glass in this window is partly medieval (the coats of arms in the upper part) and partly Victorian. In the south wall of the chancel is the priest's doorway, lavishly adorned with colonnettes when seen from the outside, and Early English piscina and sedilia. Early in the fourteenth century, two Decorated windows were inserted into the west end of the chancel, increasing the effect of spaciousness and light within.

The nave and south aisle were built later in the thirteenth century than the chancel, and the absence of a north aisle is much regretted.

(Fig 43) **St Oswald, Ashbourne** *The tower and spire.*

(Fig 44) **St Oswald, Ashbourne** *Decorated (left) and Perpendicular (right) windows in the south transept.*

(Fig 45) **St Oswald, Ashbourne** *Monument to Penelope Boothby.*

This is really the only blemish of St Oswald's, giving an asymmetrical and unfinished appearance to the body of the church. The windows in the south aisle show well the transition from Early English to Decorated: they are of three lights, under a common hood-mould externally, and there is just the germ of Decorated tracery evident in the upper part of each window (Fig.1, p.8). The piers of the south arcade have eight shafts (Fig.41), with some fine leaf capitals (Fig.42) again showing late thirteenth-century transition between Early English and Decorated.

Between the nave and chancel is the crossing where four great piers support the central tower and spire; the south-east pier previously contained a spiral staircase which led up to the balcony at the base of the recessed spire; from outside it can be seen to terminate in a short octagonal spirelet. The tower itself is very fine, and has two pairs of early Decorated windows in the belfry on each side. Above is the elegant spire, which arises to 212 feet above the ground and has twenty canopied windows in the same style as the tower (Fig.43).

The transepts are unusually wide, and are each divided by an arcade. The south transept, though basically Early English, later had two windows in the south wall: the eastern is Perpendicular, the western Decorated with intersecting tracery (Fig.44). The north transept has lancet windows in the east wall, and some of these contain some medieval stained glass. The eastern part of this transept is enclosed by a medieval oak screen and here are a fine series of monuments to members of the Cokayne, Bradbourne and Boothby families, notably the memorials to Joan and Edmund Cokayne (1404), Sir John and Lady Cokayne (1447), and Sir Humphrey and Lady Bradbourne (1581). Many of the medieval tombs are very impressive but I think for most visitors they are outshone by the memorial to six-year-old Penelope Boothby, who died in 1791 (Fig.45). During life Penelope had been painted by Sir Joshua Reynolds and in death she was immortalised by Thomas Banks, RA (1735-1805) (Esdaile). Best known for his memorials to Burgess and Westcott in St Paul's Cathedral, Banks was inspired by Penelope to portray death in childhood with an intensity and pathos which few have equalled. The anguish of the parents is movingly expressed: 'She was in form and intellect most exquisite. The unfortunate parents ventured their all on this frail bark, and the wreck was total'.

Access: St Oswald's is situated prominently just to the west of the town centre, on the A52. The church is open daily.

The Decorated Style — the fourteenth century

The Decorated style was introduced elsewhere in England around 1300, and arrived in Derbyshire somewhat later; the two great Decorated churches of the county are Chesterfield and Tideswell. Decorated arches are not so acutely pointed as in the preceding period, and the piers are more often octagonal or multi-shafted (Fig.113, p.68) than circular in cross-section. The carvings on the moulded capitals are freer and more elaborate, and when foliage is seen it is more realistic than the stiff-leaf carving of the Early English style. Around 1300 or shortly after, a development of the Y-tracery seen in the later part of the Early English period occurred in which each mullion of grouped lancets of the window branched out into two curved bars, forming so-called intersecting tracery (Figs.46 and 47). But the most characteristic feature of the Decorated style, which was to stamp its hallmark on the whole fourteenth century, was the ogee arch — two shallow S-shaped curves meeting upwards in a sharp point, and often embellished with crockets and other ornamental features (Fig.48). There was nothing functional about the ogee arch — it was an exuberant artistic fancy. In windows it led to complicated patterns of flowing tracery (Figs. 49 and 50), some of which may be described as geometrical, curvilinear or reticulated. Another character-

(Fig 48) **St Oswald, Ashbourne** *The ogee-arch.*

(Fig 47) **St Andrew, Cubley** *Intersecting tracery.*

(Fig 49) **St Mary and St Barlok, Norbury** *Decorated window tracery.*

(Fig 46) **St Michael, Breaston** *Window tracery showing evolution from Early English to Decorated styles.*

(Fig 50) **St John the Baptist, Tideswell** *Decorated window tracery.*

(Fig 51) **St John the Baptist, Dronfield** *The chancel.*

(Fig 52) **St Giles, Sandiacre** *The chancel.*

istic motif of the Decorated age was ball-flower ornamentation — a small ball enclosed by three petals forming a globular flower; this was often set in rows on a concave moulding on windows and elsewhere.

One of the notable features of fourteenth-century churches in Derbyshire is the spaciousness and quality of a small group of chancels. These include Chaddesden, Dronfield (Fig.51), Norbury (Fig.129, p.77) Sandiacre (Fig.52 and also Fig.135 p.80) Taddington and Tideswell (Fig.59, p.40).

Decorated towers were typically of four storeys; the ground floor, opening into the nave through the tower arch; above this, a ringers' gallery, with small windows; then the belfry, with prominent windows; and at the top, the roof surmounted with a spire (Fig.4, p.12). The spire at Breadsall (Fig.38, p.32) is one of the finest in the county and is recessed within a parapet, in contrast to the broach spire. Buttressing in the fourteenth and later centuries was usually diagonal, placed at the four corners of the structure.

St Mary and All Saints, Chesterfield

Chesterfield was the site of a Roman fort on Ryknield Street, and the name of the town means 'field by the Roman station'. As befits the second largest town in

Derbyshire, Chesterfield boasts the finest Gothic church in the county, known nationally because of its crooked spire (Fig.53).

There must have been a church here in Saxon or Norman times, for in 1100 William II gave the advowson to the Dean and Chapter of Lincoln. There is, however, no trace of this building, the earliest part of the present church being the piers supporting the crossing tower, and the north and south transepts. These were built in the Early English period, around 1225-1250. Most of the rest of the church was built in the Decorated style, one hundred years later.

Inside, the nave at once imparts the 'feel' of a great Decorated church (Fig.54). The piers are quatrefoil in cross-section, with hollows in the diagonals and fillets on the main shafts. Above is a Perpendicular clerestory. The Jacobean pulpit is finely carved. In the south transept is the plain Norman font, and part of the fan-vaulted sixteenth-century screen (Fig.55) separates the transept from the Lesser Lady Chapel.

The eastern end of the church is unusually complex for an English parish church, due to the proliferation of chapels sponsored by the wealth of medieval guilds. To the north of the chancel is the Holy Cross Chapel, which

(Fig 53) **St Mary and All Saints, Chesterfield** *The tower and spire.*

(Fig 54) **St Mary and All Saints, Chesterfield** *The nave and chancel arch.*

(Fig 55) **St Mary and All Saints, Chesterfield** *The Norman font and sixteenth-century screen.*

(Fig 56) **St Mary and All Saints, Chesterfield** *Tomb-chest of Sir Godfrey and Lady Foljambe (1585).*

contains a trefoiled thirteenth-century piscina; this chapel was founded by the oldest of the guilds, the Guild of Our Lady and the Holy Cross. St Katherine's Chapel, to the north of the high altar, is enclosed by the other part of the original rood-screen. To the south of the altar is the Lady Chapel, containing a series of alabaster tombs of the Foljambe family; some of these are very fine, especially that of Sir Godfrey Foljambe (Fig.56) and his wife (died 1585). Note the fine pair of brass candelabra in the Lady and St Katherine's Chapels.

Access: Thanks to the spire, the parish church in the town centre literally cannot be missed!

St John the Baptist, Tideswell

When driving along the road from Chapel-en-le-Frith to Baslow, the tower of Tideswell church can just be seen above the surrounding fields. Closer inspection reveals a parish church of the most ambitious proportions (Fig.57), set at the head of a small valley over 1,000 feet above sea level. How could such a noble church be built *here*, one wonders.

For Tideswell does not seem to have been a very important place in early medieval times.

(Fig 57) **St John the Baptist, Tideswell.**

(Fig 58) **St John the Baptist, Tideswell** *Decorated north arcade.*

(Fig 59) **St John the Baptist, Tideswell** *The chancel.*

According to Ekwall, the name means 'Tidi's stream', Tidi being a personal name. No church nor priest is mentioned in Domesday Book, and indeed at that time Tideswell was merely a hamlet in the parish of Hope; and with Hope, it was given by Prince John in 1192 to the Bishop of Coventry and Lichfield. It was not until 1254 that Tideswell became an independent parish. And then suddenly, in the next century, the present outstanding church was built, between 1340 and 1390. Prosperity must have come to Tideswell in a big way!

What is so lovely about this church is that it is all fourteenth century, Decorated throughout except the tower and west window

which came last and are clearly Perpendicular. There was a small preceding church, for the roof line of the earlier chancel can be seen inside the west wall of the present chancel. It appears that the nave, aisle and transepts were built in the 1340s, followed after an interval by the chancel, and then last of all the tower.

The nave with clerestory, aisles and transepts are all replete with Decorated window tracery, that of the south window of the south transept being the finest (Fig.50, p.37). The arcades are graceful, with piers of very complex cross-section, and finely moulded capitals (Fig.58). At the west end note the remarkably tall tower arch, and the Perpendicular west window

(Fig 60) **St John the Baptist, Tideswell** *Effigy of Sir Thurstan de Bower.*

(Fig.63, p.42). The roof has heavy tie-beams, with cusped tracery above.

The chancel (Fig.59), which is the showpiece of the church, is a marvel of light and splendour, and the great east window has flowing tracery filled with stained glass indicating the Tree of Jesse (telling the story of the genealogical descent of Jesus from Jesse, the father of David). The side windows are straight-headed, and very vertical, more Perpendicular than Decorated. The sedilia and piscina in the south wall of the chancel are ogee-headed, in the typical Decorated manner (Fig.179b, p.108), and there are also two ogee recesses in the north wall. Behind the high altar is a stone reredos enclosing a sacristy — as the church guide points out, this is most unusual in a parish church.

Of the many monuments, the best are: in the chancel, the tomb of Sir John Foljambe (died 1383), with its brass which is a copy made in 1875, the brass of Bishop Pursglove (died 1579), still showing pre-Reformation vestments, and the tomb of Sir Sampson Meverill (died 1462), which bears a brass with a symbolic representation of the Holy Trinity; and in the south transept an alabaster effigy, said to be of Sir Thurstan de Bower (died 1423; Fig 60).

Access: The church is in the centre of Tideswell, which is situated half a mile south of the A623, midway between Baslow and Chapel-en-le-Frith.

The Perpendicular Style
— 1350-1550

Bubonic plague struck England in 1348-1350, and the Black Death wiped out a quarter, perhaps a third, of the population. It is a tribute to the faith in medieval times that, in this ghastly fourteenth century, when plague was compounded by bad harvests and disaster occurred on a scale never known in England before or since, there was no pause in church building in many counties. In Cheshire, for example, there was a notable surge of building between 1350 and 1400, and later, in the fifteenth century, all the noblest medieval churches in Cheshire were completed (Nantwich, Bunbury, Astbury, Malpas, Great Budworth). In Derbyshire, however, there is not a single church which could now reasonably be called Perpendicular*. Many churches had attention to towers, roofs and windows, but there is a complete dearth of whole buildings built in the Perpendicular style. Why is this?

(Fig 61) **St Giles, Great Longstone** *Perpendicular roof and clerestory.*

The answer, must, I think, lie in the economic circumstances of the county during the fifteenth century. At a time when there was great prosperity in other parts of the country, for example East Anglia, and noble Perpendicular churches were constructed on the most ambitious scale, Derbyshire remained relatively poor, and probably the population failed to grow after the Black Death. So all that was needed, or could be afforded, was relatively small-scale amendments to the existing buildings.

Towers were often heightened, and received battlements and pinnacles. The steeply sloping roofs of earlier centuries were replaced by low-pitched roofs; this enabled the side walls of the naves to be heightened, thus allowing for the insertion of a clerestory (Fig.61), which now became the rule for parish churches and brought a welcome increase in light. Perpendicular windows, often the straight-headed variety known as Tudor windows (Fig.62), were frequently inserted into the walls of naves, aisles and chancels of previous buildings.

(Fig 62) **St Mary, Denby** *Straight-headed 'Tudor' windows, fourteenth-century broach spire.*

(Fig 63) **St John the Baptist, Tideswell** *Perpendicular tower arch and west window. Tie-beam roof.*

The Perpendicular style prevailed in England for 200 years (*c*.1350-1550), persisting until the Reformation. The emphasis throughout is on verticality; straight lines replace the sinuous tracery of the Decorated period; the pointed arches become flatter. This 'alters the proportions of the arcade: a larger part of its height is now taken up by the piers. The piers being both taller and thinner make the arcade appear loftier and produce the impression of height (Fig.63) and lightness of structure that is so characteristic of the Perpendicular style. . . . The preference for straight lines shows particularly clearly in window tracery. There the vertical mullions that divide a window into its lights rise almost without interruption to the head of the window (Fig.64), ruling its tracery into tiers of rectangular compartments.' (Foster, p.161).

* I am indebted to the Reverend John Drackley for pointing out that the old Derby churches of All Saints, St Michael and St Alkmund were probably built in the Perpendicular style.

(Fig 64) **All Saints, Breadsall** *Perpendicular east window.*

Other Medieval Churches

(Fig 66) **All Saints, Ashover** *The lead font.*

All Saints, Ashover

This is one of the outstanding village churches in Derbyshire (Fig.65), with plenty to interest the observant visitor. It is of national importance because of the lead font (Fig.66) — there are said to be only 30 of these in the country. It is not surprising that this font, which is the oldest object in the church and which dates from the twelfth century, should be here, because lead has been mined in the area from Roman times. On the bowl are carved standing figures, said to represent the Apostles, under a series of arcades.

The oldest part of the church is the south porch (Fig.67), which was built in the Early English style in the second half of the thirteenth century. Stepping inside into the nave, the visitor is immediately struck by the contrast between the north and south arcades. On the left, the north arcade is Decorated, with octagonal piers and plain capitals; on the right, the south arcade is Perpendicular, with much taller and slenderer piers. The chancel is also Decorated, with ogee-headed north and south doorways, and the two trefoiled recesses in the north wall, one of which may have been an Easter sepulchre before the Reformation. (This

(Fig 67) **All Saints, Ashover** *The porch.*

(Fig 68) **All Saints, Ashover** *Tomb of Thomas Babington and his wife (1518).*

would house the consecrated Host from Maundy Thursday until Easter Day.) The windows in the chancel are all later

Perpendicular insertions. Notice the fine rood-screen between the nave and chancel; this dates from the early sixteenth century. In the Perpendicular age also came the clerestory and the west tower (although the belfry windows still have Decorated tracery; the date of the tower is said to be 1419).

Within the chancel are two very fine sixteenth-century brasses, to Philip Eyre and to James Rolleston and his wife Anna, respectively. But the finest monument in Ashover is the Babington alabaster tomb (Fig.68), dated 1511.

The Babingtons played a prominent part in the history of the area after Thomas Babington returned from the war, having fought at the battle of Agincourt in 1415. He came from East Bridgford in Nottinghamshire, and married the heiress of Dethick in the parish of Ashover, thus becoming the lord of Dethick (q.v.). As Dethick church had no rights of burial, he and his heirs were buried at Ashover, and the later Thomas Babington who died in 1518 gave the fine rood-screen to the church. The Babington tomb, said by Pevsner to be the best of its date in Derbyshire,

(Fig 65) **All Saints, Ashover.**

has effigies of Thomas and his wife Edith, and on the side, representations of saints, angels and mourners.

Access: From Matlock, take A632 towards Chesterfield; after nearly four miles, turn right into B6036 for Ashover. The church is on the left.

(Fig 69) **All Saints, Aston-upon-Trent.**

All Saints, Aston-upon-Trent

The church at Aston-upon-Trent (Fig.69) is worth visiting because it contains examples of every style of medieval building from Anglo-Saxon to Perpendicular; so perhaps it is best described chronologically.

The Saxon work consists of masonry at the west end of the north aisle, where a column of long-and-short work may be discerned, and above it some Saxon carving with interlace which is probably a portion of an ancient cross (Fig.3, p.10). The Norman twelfth century contributed the lower parts of the tower, with the west door, the window above, and higher still late Norman windows with nook-shafts and zigzag decoration. The tower arch into the nave is also Norman.

The arcades separating the nave from the aisles are Early English: circular piers, octagonal capitals, pointed arches. The chancel arch and the arches separating the chancel from the north chapel are also of this period (Fig.70). The south windows in the chancel and south aisle are Decorated (fourteenth century) with some unusual features. In the chancel, the south windows are remarkably tall, with Decorated tracery both above and below the horizontal transom. In the easternmost window of the

south aisle are ogee-headed canopies in the jambs on each side. In the Perpendicular period, the tower was completed with battlements, and a clerestory was added to the nave. There is one notable monument in the north aisle — an alabaster tomb with effigies of a man and wife clasping hands, she with a small dog lying at her feet; on the side are angels bearing shields.

Access: From Derby, take the A6 south towards Loughborough; the turning to Aston is on the right, just after Thulston. On entering the village, keep straight on past the road to Weston, and the church will be found on the right-hand side.

(Fig 70) **All Saints, Aston-upon-Trent** *Early English arcade and chancel arch.*

(Fig 71) **St John the Baptist, Ault Hucknall.**

St John the Baptist, Ault Hucknall

One of the finest village churches in Derbyshire, it is pleasantly situated in countryside a short way from industrial areas, and has much to interest the visitor.

The name of the village is an unusual compound of French and Old English; it shares the second component with Hucknall Torkard, eleven miles away in Nottinghamshire; Ault (previously Hault) is from the French *haut* (high), and Torkard is a French family name. Hucknall is believed to be the name of a large district, meaning Hucca's valley, and in between the two Hucknalls is Huthwaite, which used to be named Hucknall under Huthwaite (Ekwall).

Unusually for a village church, St John's is of cruciform shape, with a central crossing and tower (Fig.71). The west arch of the crossing, facing the nave, is Norman, ornamented with carvings said to illustrate scenes from the book of Genesis. The east arch of the crossing, opening into the chancel, is exceedingly narrow and plain, and is claimed by some to be of Saxon origin (Fig.72). Pevsner is not quite convinced, but certainly attributes it to the late eleventh century.

The nave and north aisle are also early Norman, the rectangular pier being very plain; in contrast the south aisle is Early English (thirteenth century). The upper parts of the crossing tower, the battlements, the vaulted south porch and the south chapel are all Perpendicular. In this chapel are buried the great philosopher Thomas Hobbes and Ann, first countess of Devonshire. Above her tomb is a fine window dated 1527 (the Savage window) portraying the Crucifixion with the Virgin Mary and St John, and on the far right St Ursula. The Savage family held the local manor of Stainsby for 300 years. The tomb of the Countess of Devonshire is surmounted by five alabaster figures, representing, according to the inscription, Modesty, Prudence, Love, Obedience and Piety.

I have left until last perhaps the most remarkable object in this fascinating church — the Norman tympanum and lintel in the west wall externally (Fig.24, p.23). The lintel portrays St George and the dragon, separated by a cross, while in the tympanum above is carved the legend of St Margaret of Antioch. Keyser describes it as follows: 'Here is an animal with the claws, long neck and head of a bird, and with a long tail wound under the body, and terminating above it in a cross within a circle (the lamb of God). Facing this is . . .an animal with the head thrown back, and the bust of a female figure emerging from its body, and holding a cross in one hand and a palm in the other. Here undoubtedly we have the legend of St Margaret emerging from the body of the Evil One, who had swallowed her, 'through the power of the Cross'.'

Access: Ault Hucknall is four miles south of Bolsover. From Exit 29 of the M1 take the A6175 towards Clay Cross, and after a short distance turn into the first lane on the left. This runs alongside the motorway for a while, and then a turning on the left leads under the motorway to Ault Hucknall one mile distant. The church is on the left, and the key to it may be obtained from the house opposite.

(Fig 72) **St John the Baptist, Ault Hucknall** *West and east arches of the crossing.*

All Saints, Bakewell

Bakewell, perhaps the most characteristic of Derbyshire market towns, has an ancient history. It first featured in the Anglo-Saxon Chronicle in 924, when King Edward went 'into Peakland, to Bakewell, and commanded a castle to be built nigh there unto, and garrisoned'. This was during the Anglo-Saxon reconquest of Derbyshire from the Danes. Bakewell was clearly thenceforth of some significance, and by the time of the Domesday survey (1086) it was described as possessing not only a church but *two* priests — a most unusual distinction. No trace remains of any Saxon church, but there is the Saxon cross in the churchyard and in the porch and against the west wall of the church are a large number of Saxon and Norman fragments discovered during excavations in the nineteenth century; these may well relate to earlier buildings.

Bakewell church stands imposingly on a hillside above the town and is clearly an impressive building, with its octagonal tower and spire (Fig.2, p.9). The oldest part of the church is the west front, which is Norman, as shown by the round-headed west doorway (Fig.73) with two orders of colonnettes, and arches decorated with beakhead and saltire crosses. Inside the west front are blocked Norman arches (Fig.74) which were originally intended to be entrances into two west towers (cf Melbourne), a project which never materialised. The first bay of each arcade is also Norman, with the round arches contrasting with the Gothic arches of the remainder of the arcades which in fact were reconstructed in 1852. Also at the west end note the fourteenth-century

(Fig 73) **All Saints, Bakewell** *The west door.*

font (Fig.75) with carved figures under ogee arches.

The chancel and south transept are Early English (though the latter was completely rebuilt between 1841 and 1852); the two east windows of the chancel consist of twin lancets,

(Fig 74) **All Saints, Bakewell** *North aisle, showing the blocked Norman arch.*

(Fig 76) **All Saints, Bakewell** *Monument to Sir Godfrey and Lady Foljambe (1385).*

(Fig 75) **All Saints, Bakewell** *Fourteenth-century font.*

with Y-tracery typical of the late thirteenth century (Fig.37, p.31). Note the sedilia and piscina in the south wall of the chancel (Fig.176b, p.107). In the same century was built the lower stage of the tower, the octagonal upper stage, the battlements and spire following in the next century. In the Perpendicular age (fifteenth century) came the south porch, the clerestory, and the north window of the north transept.

The monuments in Bakewell church are of considerable interest, the finest and most unusual being the unique wall monument to Sir Godfrey Foljambe and his wife dating from 1385, and placed between the south aisle and the nave. The two alabaster figures are shown from the waist up, side by side, beneath an elaborate ogee-shaped canopy (Fig.76). In the east aisle of the south transept are memorials to the Vernons of Haddon Hall (other and finer Vernon tombs are in the grand church of Tong, Shrophsire), to Dorothy Vernon and her husband Sir John Manners, and to Sir George Manners.

Access: Up a short hill, just to the west of the town centre. The church is open daily.

St Mary, Bolsover

Bolsover parish church has been most unlucky, having been severely damaged by fire twice within the last century (1897 and 1960). Fortunately, after the second conflagration, the opportunity was taken to reorganise the arrangements for worship to good effect, and the result is very pleasing and worth seeing.

After the Norman Conquest, Bolsover was granted by the King to William of Peveril, and it was probably he or his son who founded both the church and the castle. Of the Norman church there remains only the rather weather-worn tympanum above the south chancel door; this shows the Crucifixion, flanked by the figures of the Virgin Mary and St John (Fig.23, p.23). The Early English tower, with broach spire, escaped harm in both the fires. On the east wall of the north aisle is a marvellous piece of medieval sculpture; though somewhat damaged, it can be seen to represent the Adoration of the Magi (Fig.77). The origin of this slab is unknown: it was discovered in 1704 in the north door of the church, where, face down, it had served as a step (Cox).

To the south of the chancel is the Cavendish chapel, built in 1618, and containing two outstanding monuments. The earlier commemorates Sir Charles Cavendish (died 1617) and his wife. The fine alabaster effigy of Sir Charles lies above and behind that of his wife (Fig.78), and below are shown their three sons kneeling. From the eighteenth century, there is the memorial to Henry Cavendish, Duke of Newcastle, his wife and daughter. Pevsner describes it as follows: '. . .a very civilised marble monument of reredos type, with a big, black, sarcophagus between large coupled Corinthian columns supporting a pediment on which lie two allegorical figures.'

Access: Bolsover is on the A632, about six miles east of Chesterfield. Proceed up the hill past the castle to the town centre, and then shortly after the main road takes a sharp turn to the right, St Mary's will be found on the right.

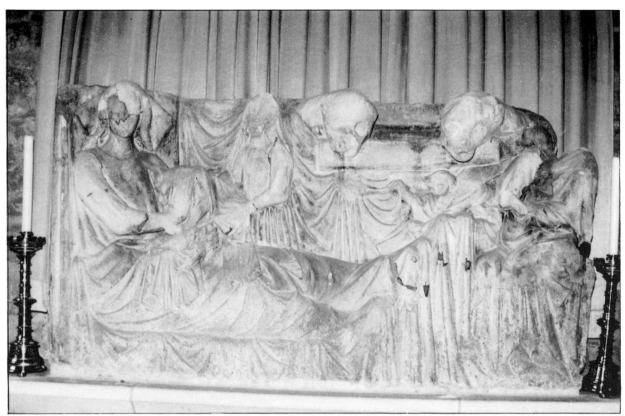

(Fig 77) **St Mary, Bolsover** *Thirteenth-century sculpture of the Adoration of the Magi.*

(Fig 78) **St Mary, Bolsover** *Monument to Sir Charles and Lady Cavendish (1617).*

All Saints, Bradbourne

Bradbourne is one of those churches which are definitely more interesting outside than in. To begin with, it is nicely situated next to the old parsonage and hall, with very pleasant countryside beyond. Then there is, in the churchyard, an ancient Saxon cross, dated to *c*.800 (Fig.9, p.16). The church existed in Saxon times, for it is mentioned in Domesday Book, and there is some Saxon long-and-short work visible at the eastern end of the north wall of the nave.

But perhaps the greatest attraction of Bradbourne is the Norman tower, with its ornate south door. The tower is short and rather squat, and the twin bell-openings are surmounted by a Norman rounded arch decorated with zigzag and billet mouldings. Above this can be seen the original Norman corbel- table, just below the later battlements (Fig.79). It is, however, the south door of the tower which catches the eye: over the door are three arches, the inner two carved with bird and animal shapes, the outer one being decorated with beakhead (Fig.80).

In 1205, the church was given to the Prior of Dunstable, and the church was enlarged shortly afterwards. So inside, the tower opens into the nave through a rounded Norman tower arch, and there are Early English lancet windows in the north side of the nave and chancel. The south arcade is later, *c*.1300, and in the Decorated style, with the piers quatrefoil in cross-section. The chancel arch is said to be later fourteenth century.

Access: From Ashbourne, proceed north along the Buxton road (A515), and after two miles turn right into B5056 towards Matlock. The road to Bradbourne is on the right after three miles, and the church is at the beginning of the village on the left.

(Fig 80) **All Saints, Bradbourne** *The south door of the tower, with rather worn beakhead decoration in the outer order of the arch.*

(Fig 79) **All Saints, Bradbourne**

(Fig 81) **All Saints, Brailsford.**

All Saints, Brailsford

Brailsford church commands a lovely situation, isolated among fields about half a mile from the village (Fig.81). The reason for this is that it was originally built in the eleventh or twelfth century to serve both the manors of Brailsford and Ednaston (Ednodestun), each of which is described in Domesday Book as having half a church; and indeed All Saints is equidistant from the two villages.

When I visited Brailsford in March, the churchyard was a mass of daffodils, and earlier had been alive with snowdrops and crocuses. The Saxon cross (Fig.11, p.17) has already been described.

The building itself consists of a nave and chancel, south aisle and tower. The arcade separating the nave and south aisle is unusual: the westernmost pier is clearly Norman, with a scalloped capital, and to the west a rounded arch connects with the west wall embracing the tower, proving, as Pevsner points out, that the tower was built into the width of the Norman nave. The other piers of the arcade are later, one circular, the other octagonal, yet all the arches are round and, if original, would indicate a date towards the end of the twelfth century. There is a further obvious Norman pier supporting the north side of the much later

(fourteenth century) chancel arch (Fig.82). In the south wall of the chancel are a plain set of late thirteenth-century sedilia and piscina (Fig.176c, p.107). Notice the attractive carving in the bench ends of the pews in the nave (Fig.171, p.105). The octagonal font is late Perpendicular, the lower part of the base exhibiting the Tudor rose.

Access: Brailsford is on the A52, slightly nearer to Ashbourne than to Derby. From Derby, proceed through the village and then take a lane on the left which is signposted 'Brailsford Church'. After a few hundred yards, turn right down a track which leads to the church.

(Fig 82) **All Saints, Brailsford** *The Norman arcade and fourteenth-century chancel arch.*

(Fig 83) **St James, Brassington** *Norman capitals with leaf and scallop design.*

(Fig 84) **St James, Brassington** *Norman arcade.*

St James, Brassington

In medieval times, Brassington was a chapelry of Bradbourne, and with Bradbourne was given to the Priory of Dunstable which held it until the Reformation. Later Brassington became a separate parish but in recent years has been re-united with Bradbourne.

The church is worth seeing because of the fine Norman south arcade which separates the narrow south aisle from the nave. Most unusually, there is also an arcade separating the chancel from a south chancel chapel. In the nave, the piers are massive and circular, with large square capitals carved with the scallop design, the middle one also showing leaves (Fig.83). The pier supporting the arcade between the chancel and chapel is a little later, being octagonal and again with leaf design (Fig.84). The tower arch is rounded and Norman, and contrasts with the Decorated chancel arch.

Externally, the west tower is Norman and the south porch thirteenth century.

Access: From Ashbourne, take the B5035 north-east towards Wirksworth, and the turning to Brassington is about 5½ miles to the left. The church is in a prominent position overlooking the village.

St Edmund, Castleton

The dedication of this church is to the King of East Anglia who was martyred by the Danes in 869, five years before the sack of Repton and Breedon. Church and village now nestle below the ruins of the castle of William de Peveril, who in Norman times was granted extensive lands in this region. He was also William 1's bailiff for the manors of Hope, Bakewell and Ashford, and in the passage of time acquired all these. Throughout the twelfth century, the church remained in the hands of William Peveril and his descendants until one of them poisoned his mistress' husband, the Earl of Chester, and the lands were then forfeited to the Crown. In 1269, Castleton was given by Prince Edward (later Edward I) to Dernall Abbey, in Cheshire, and later passed into the hands of Vale Royal Abbey. At the Reformation, it was transferred to the Bishop of Chester.

The church certainly dates back to Norman times, as shown by the very impressive chancel arch, adorned with chevron moulding (Fig.85). Unfortunately, most of the rest of the building

(Fig 85) **St Edmund, Castleton** *Norman chancel arch.*

dates from the restoration in the early nineteenth century. The tower, however, is an attractive late Perpendicular edifice, surmounted with battlements and pinnacles and with diagonal buttresses.

The nave is filled with a fine series of seventeenth-century box-pews, some of which bear the names of parishioners of those days (Fig.86). Samuel Cryer was the vicar from 1644-1697.

Access: Castleton is on the A625 Sheffield to Chapel-en-le-Frith road, but this road is blocked at Mam Tor, just west of the village. From Chapel, take the A6 and then A623 towards Chesterfield, and then turn left on B6049 through Bradwell to reach the A625.

(Fig 86) **St Edmund, Castleton** *Seventeenth-century box-pews.*

St Michael and All Angels, Church Broughton

This is pastoral Derbyshire, and St Michael's is a nice Decorated church (Fig.87) set in an attractive village. Two of the Auden family were vicars here from 1864-1933; the poet W.H.Auden visited his relatives here as a boy. (Incidentally, his first Christian name was Wystan, the patron saint of Repton.)

The excellent church guide provides an interesting history of the village and church. St Michael's appears to have been founded in the twelfth century, when the village was included in gifts by the grandson of Henry de Ferrers to the priory of Tutbury. The arcades are Decorated, of the fourteenth century, with circular piers and moulded capitals. However, if you look carefully at the half-pillar at the eastern end of the north arcade, you will see that it has a square capital, with Norman scalloping under it (Fig.88) — a clear vestige of an earlier Norman church. The only other relic of the twelfth century is the Norman font, adorned with geometrical triangles and circles, said to symbolise the Trinity and Eternity. At the western end of the arcades the first pier on each side is elongated; these are thought to date from the fourteenth-century rebuilding when the tower was added, requiring an extra bay for the nave. On each pillar is a grotesque carving of a man's and a woman's head respectively.

The chancel arch is graceful, with leaf carving under the capitals. The chancel itself is Decorated throughout, with a good east window and ogee-canopied sedilia and piscina

(Fig 88) **St Michael, Church Broughton** *Decorated chancel arch and east window. Norman capital with scallop to left of chancel arch.*

(Fig.177a, p.107). The tower also is Decorated, with a recessed spirelet. In the Perpendicular period, the height of the nave was raised to permit the insertion of a clerestory, and the pitch of the roof was lowered. A straight-headed Perpendicular window was also inserted in the south wall of the chancel.

Access: From Derby, take the A38 south, and then the A516 west through Etwall and Hilton. This road then joins the A50 to Uttoxeter. The turning to Church Broughton is on the right, just over a mile after the junction with A50. The church is in the north of the village.

(Fig 87) **St Michael, Church Broughton** *Decorated tower.*

St Mary, Crich

Crich comes from a British word 'cruc' meaning a hill (cf Crichel Down in Dorset), and the area, like Wirksworth on the other side of the Derwent Valley, was an ancient site of lead mining, and mentioned as such in Domesday Book. From the outside, the church appears to be mainly fourteenth century, but the interior tells a different story.

For the arcades are clearly twelfth-century Norman, with substantial cylindrical piers supporting round arches and displaying square capitals, some of which are adorned with scallop carving. The south arcade is somewhat later than the north, the capitals being rounded and not square. The next major work is in the Decorated style of the fourteenth century; at the east end of each arcade a narrow pointed arch connects with the new work in the chancel arch, chancel and aisles (Fig.89). The east window in the chancel is of five lights, with reticulated tracery above. Also in the chancel, note the built-in bible-rest made of stone; a few of these are known in Derbyshire, but they are exceedingly rare elsewhere. A good incised slab to German Pole and his wife is also present in the chancel wall (Fig.90). The west tower, recessed spire, clerestory and south porch are later still, being Perpendicular work of the fifteenth century.

Much of the fourteenth-century work is thought to be due to the beneficence of Sir William de Wakebridge, who endowed a chantry chapel in the north aisle. In a recess in this aisle is an effigy of the late fourteenth century, presumed to be Sir William's. His story is reminiscent of the sufferings of Job: in 1348 the Black Death arrived, and within three months this wealthy local squire lost his father, wife, three brothers, two sisters and a sister-in-law. Henceforth he appears to have given up himself to good works, and especially to the extension of St Mary's church.

Access: From Matlock, take the A6 southwards, and after about seven miles the road to Crich (B5035) is on the left. In the centre of Crich, turn left where the main road bends right, and the church is on the right.

(Fig 90) **St Mary, Crich** *Incised alabaster slab to German Pole and his wife (1588).*

(Fig 89) **St Mary, Crich** *The chancel arch and east window.*

St Andrew, Cubley

St Andrew's is a very attractive village church a few miles south of Ashbourne. The church goes back a long way, being mentioned in Domesday Book, and the earliest part of the church is Norman. Indeed, there is some herringbone masonry in the north wall of the nave which could even be of Saxon origin.

The arcade separating the south aisle from the nave is late twelfth century, with circular piers and rounded arches (Fig.91); one capital is octagonal, and carved with a leaf motif. The font is also Norman. The piers supporting the chancel arch are Norman, but the pointed arch itself is a later insertion, probably thirteenth century. The chancel is Early English, with lancet windows in the north and south walls. The east window of the chancel is a later fourteenth-century addition, showing Decorated intersecting tracery (restored in 1872; Fig.47, p.36). There are two alabaster tomb-chests in the chancel, one to Sir Nicholas Montgomery (died 1235) and the second to a later knight of the same name who died in 1494. These tombs were originally of high quality, but they have been sadly defaced. The tower

(Fig 91) **St Andrew, Cubley** *Norman arcade, Early English chancel arch and Decorated east window.*

is late Perpendicular, with an embattled parapet with pinnacles; on the exterior walls are ten coats of arms. Lastly, the seventeenth century contributed the square-headed windows in the nave and south aisle, those on the north side being larger.

Access: From Ashbourne, take the A515 south towards Lichfield. After about six miles, turn left for Cubley.

All Saints, Dale Abbey

This enchanting little church is possibly the only semi-detached church in the country (Fig.92), and has a lot to offer the visitor.

The village of Dale Abbey grew up around the Abbey, which was re-founded as a Premonstratensian monastery *c.*1198. The monastery was dissolved in 1538 and passed into lay hands, and then into ruin. It is possible

(Fig 92) **All Saints, Dale Abbey.**

(Fig 93) **All Saints, Dale Abbey** *Medieval wall-painting, old pews and leaning pulpit.*

(Fig 94) **All Saints, Dale Abbey** *Ancient timbers and box-pews.*

that the existing church of All Saints was previously the infirmary of the abbey — certainly some of the masonry appears to date back to the twelfth century, and there is a painting on the north wall which has been dated to the thirteenth century (Fig.93). The building became a parish church after the dissolution of the monastery.

Externally, All Saints shares the same roof with a farm, which used to be an inn. Internally it is essentially a seventeenth-century chapel, with the oddest assembly of box-pews, a leaning pulpit dated 1634 and a reading desk (both behind the altar), a Jacobean cupboard used as a Communion table, a gallery, and ancient oak timbers (Fig.94). It still contains the abbey font, dating from the fifteenth century.

Access: Regular services are held at the church, which, together with the adjacent Abbey ruins, is open at any reasonable time. Refreshments may be available at the Gateway Christian Centre in the village, which used to be the Methodist church. From Derby, take the A6096 north-eastwards towards Ilkeston; the turning to Dale Abbey is on the right, about two miles after leaving the outskirts of Derby.

St John the Baptist, Dethick

It is conjectured that Dethick means 'death oak', i.e. an oak on which felons were hanged' (Ekwall); if so, it seems an appropriate name for a place which came under the ownership of the ill-fated Babington family. The manor of Dethick was first recorded in 1202 and was under the ownership of the family that took their name from the manor for two hundred years. Then the male line of the Dethick family failed because of the death at the Battle of Shrewsbury (1403) of Robert Dethick and his son and heir, Thomas. The heiress, Isabella Dethick married Thomas Babington, and the Babington family held the estate until 1635.

The church has a fine situation on high ground south of Matlock (Fig.95), and is in close proximity to Manor Farm, Babington Farm and Church Farm, the whole complex being a group of listed buildings. The building dates back to the thirteenth century, as evidenced by the original small lancet windows. Sir Anthony Babington in 1530 built the Perpendicular tower, which is the outstanding feature of the church, and also heightened the nave by providing a clerestory. The tower arch into the nave is very tall and narrow. Externally, the tower has diagonal buttresses, battlements, and a south-east stair-turret. The west front has Perpendicular windows, and all round the tower below the bell-openings is a frieze of carved heraldic shields belonging to the families with which the Babingtons had intermarried, some of which have already featured in these pages; these include the Ferrers, Rollastons and Fitzherberts.

Disaster struck the Babington family in 1586 when Antony Babington, grandson of the man who enlarged the church, was implicated in a plot to free Mary, Queen of Scots and to murder Queen Elizabeth. Mary had been in English custody since 1568, and had spent many years in prison in and around Derbyshire, most notably at Tutbury, just over the border in Staffordshire. In 1586, Mary was at Chartley Hall, between Uttoxeter and Stafford. Letters relating to the plot were intercepted by Elizabeth's secret service run by Sir Francis Walsingham; Babington was executed in September, 1586, and Mary five months later.

(Fig 95) **St John the Baptist, Dethick.**

His estates at Dethick would have been forfeited to the Crown had he not handed them over to his younger brother before the fatal involvement with treason.

Dethick church remains today as a reminder of those grim events; when I visited it on a grey day, with driving wind and gusts of rain, it was not difficult for the imagination to run riot on gunpowder, treason and plot. But on a fine day, Dethick is a grand place for an excursion.

Access: From Matlock, proceed south along A6 to Cromford; then turn left at Cromford Wharf, and immediately after crossing the river, fork right and follow the east bank of the Derwent for a mile. The road then climbs, and at the top of the hill fork left, then bear left again, and then take the road on the right for Dethick. The church is down a short lane on the right, hidden by the farms. Please do not park on the approach road to the church. The key is at the dairy in Manor Farm.

St Peter and St Paul, Eckington

Eckington is now a large, rather sprawling industrial village set in what must once have been attractive rolling countryside, just far enough away from Chesterfield and Sheffield to have a life of its own. The village is, however, of great antiquity, being recorded in Domesday Book (1086) as Echintune and described as possessing a mill. No church is mentioned, but the earliest part of the fabric of SS. Peter and Paul must date from about a hundred years later.

The tower is arresting — a solid, noble Norman enterprise (Fig.96) with a complex west door (Fig.97), round-arched in the Norman fashion, with three orders of colonnettes at each side. Above are Early English lancet windows dating from the early thirteenth century — two immediately above the west door, one in the next stage, and three on each side of the bell-chamber. Above is a fourteenth-century recessed spire without battlements. A little incongruously, the south porch and south aisle date from the eighteenth century.

The interior is impressive, the solidity of the Norman arcades being second in Derbyshire

(Fig 96) **St Peter and St Paul, Eckington** *Early thirteenth-century tower.*

(Fig 97) **St Peter and St Paul, Eckington** *The west door.*

(Fig 98) **St Peter and St Paul, Eckington** *The interior looking west.*

only to Melbourne. The arcades are of five bays, the three easternmost piers being circular in cross-section, the two to the west being a little later and octagonal (Fig.98). All the arches are semicircular, however, pointing to a building date late in the twelfth century. The pier nearest the chancel in the north arcade has a capital with waterleaf moulding. The chancel arch itself is later than the arcades, being Early English.

In the chancel are a number of fairly undistinguished memorials to the Sitwell family, who still reside at Renishaw Hall nearby. The present owner is Sir Reresby Sitwell, seventh baronet and lord of the manors of Eckington and Barlborough. It was at Renishaw that the three writers and poets of the previous generation, Edith, Osbert and Sacheverell Sitwell were brought up; Sir Osbert wrote of the family's childhood at Renishaw Hall with undisguised nostalgia.

Access: From Chesterfield, take the A61 north towards Sheffield. At the second roundabout at Whittington Moor turn right on to B6052, and Eckington is five miles along this road. The parish church is at the far end of the village, on the left side just before the junction with the A616.

St Lawrence, Eyam

Tourists flock to Eyam (Fig.99) because of the well-known story of the heroic behaviour of the villagers during the Plague in 1665-66. The rector, William Mompesson and his puritan predecessor Thomas Stanley, persuaded the villagers to put themselves in voluntary isolation for months, during which time some 350 villagers (out of a population of c.850) died. There is a most interesting exhibition telling this story displayed in the church.

In the churchyard is an eighteenth-century sundial (Fig.100), but more important is an Anglo-Saxon cross dating from a thousand years earlier (Fig.10, p.16); it has therefore been suggested that there was probably a Saxon church here, though it is not mentioned in Domesday Book. Nor is there now any trace of a Norman building, though there is a good Norman font carved with blank arcades on columns (Fig.25, p.23). So the earliest part of the church is the Early English chancel, with lancet windows, and the north arcade of the same period. Supporting this arcade is one circular pier and one which is quatrefoil in cross-section (Fig.101). The south arcade is later, fifteenth-century Perpendicular, contemporary with the clerestory, the roof of the nave, and the west tower. There is an interesting series of wall-paintings between the clerestory windows and above the tower and chancel arches; these are not medieval, but date from the late sixteenth and seventeenth centuries and represent the twelve tribes of Israel, with later work consisting of the Creed and Lord's prayer. These paintings were covered with plaster and lost for two hundred years until galleries were removed in 1868; they were then re-covered to protect them from exposure to the light, and were not finally unveiled until 1963.

Not all the seventeenth-century incumbents of Eyam were of the same stamp as Stanley and Mompesson. They were succeeded by Mr Hunt, who, when drunk one night in the local hostelry, 'married' the landlord's daughter in a mock ceremony, and notwithstanding the fact that he was already betrothed to another

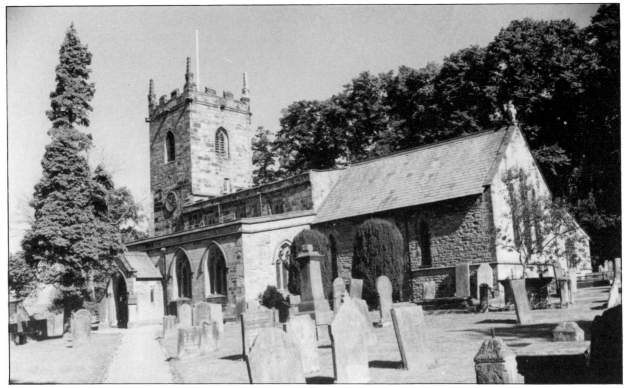

(Fig 99) **St Lawrence, Eyam.**

(Fig 100) **St Lawrence, Eyam** *Eighteenth-century sundial.*

(Fig 101) **St Lawrence, Eyam** *Early English arcade and post-Reformation wall paintings.*

young lady. Following this, he had to get wed properly in church, and was then promptly sued for breach of promise by the family of his jilted fiancée. Whereupon he took sanctuary in the church for years, building for himself, his wife and six children a little room adjacent to the thirteenth-century chancel.

Access: Eyam is half a mile north of the A623 (Chapel-en-le-Frith to Chesterfield road), about one mile west of Stoney Middleton.

St Edmund, Fenny Bentley

Most visitors to the little church at Fenny Bentley come to see the famous shrouded effigies, but these are really a curiosity and not much more. Infinitely more worth seeing is the early sixteenth-century screen, which, though somewhat restored, displays much intricate carving (Figs.102 and 103). The vaulted cornice has a flowing pattern of vine leaves and grapes. A similar parclose screen encloses the Beresford chapel.

The shrouded effigies (Fig.104) com-

(Figs 102 & 103) **St Edmund, Fenny Bentley** *The screen, the finest in Derbyshire.*

(Fig 103)

(Fig 104) **St Edmund, Fenny Bentley** *The shrouded Beresford effigies.*

memorate Thomas Beresford (died 1473) and his wife, and were apparently not executed until long after their deaths. Thomas Beresford fought with Henry V on St Crispin's day at Agincourt (1415). Shrouded representations of their sixteen sons and five daughters are incised on the south side and east end of the tomb.

The church itself has Decorated windows in the south aisle and chancel. The north aisle, fine hammer-beam roof and spire are Victorian.

Access: From Ashbourne, proceed north along A5151 towards Buxton. The turning to Fenny Bentley is on the left, after about two and a half miles. The church is just on the left.

St Giles, Great Longstone

Longstone was originally one of the chapelries of Bakewell, and with that church was given by King John to the Dean and Chapter of Lichfield in 1200. At about the same time, the king bestowed the manor of Ashford (which included Longstone) on to a Welshman named Wenuwyn. His son, Griffin, founded chantry chapels at Ashford and Longstone in 1257 and 1262 respectively, so there must have been a church at Longstone in the thirteenth century. The chantry chapel has disappeared, but there survive remnants of

(Fig 105) **St Giles, Great Longstone** *Early English door, with fine iron-work.*

the Early English church. These include the lancet windows in the north aisle, the doorway (Fig.105) inside the south porch, and the lower part of the tower.

But essentially, and ignoring for a moment the Victorian restoration, St Giles is a building of the Decorated and Perpendicular ages. The arcades and chancel arch are Decorated (Fig.106), with octagonal piers and plain capitals. The clerestory, upper part of the tower with its battlements, and most of the windows are Perpendicular.

The roof of the nave (Fig.61, p.42) could perhaps be claimed to be the finest in Derbyshire. It is a Perpendicular collar-braced oak roof of low pitch, with bosses at the intersections of the beams. Some of these are carved into foliage and flower patterns, and others show armorial bearings.

The oak parclose screen enclosing the Lady Chapel at the east end of the south aisle is also fine.

In the nave are a series of fine hatchments (or achievements); these commemorate members of local families and were popular in the period 1660-1800. They show a coat of arms on a lozenge-shaped frame. The background varies according to the marital state of the deceased. The rules are as follows: *Black background:* bachelor: arms single; spinster: arms single and lozenge-shaped; widower: arms divided into two; widow: arms divided into two and lozenge-shaped. *Half-black and half-white background:* married man dies before his wife — left side (as you look at it) black and right side white; married woman dies before her husband — left side white and right side black (Jones).

Access: From Bakewell, take the A6 north to Ashford-in-the-Water, and then turn right into A6020. After one mile, turn left for Great Longstone; the church is at the north end of the village, a short distance along a side road on the right.

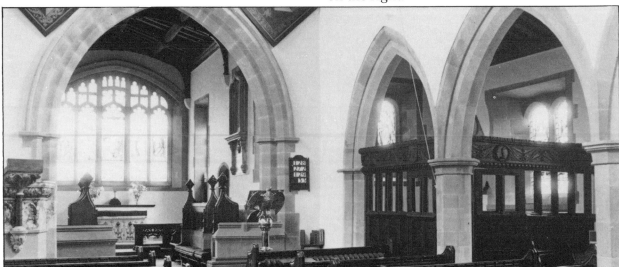

(Fig 106) **St Giles, Great Longstone** *Decorated chancel arch and arcade, Perpendicular east window and parclose screen.*

St Giles, Hartington

The name means 'stags' hill', and the little town stands on a hillside just to the east of the river Dove. Its attractive market square, complete with pond, are overlooked by St Giles' church and are a favoured resort of tourists. The manor of Hartington was held by de Ferrers at the time of the Domesday Survey but on the attainder of Robert de Ferrers in the reign of Edward I, it was annexed to the Duchy of Lancaster.

The church (Fig.107) is cruciform in shape, but without a central tower, this being at the west end. The oldest part of the building is Early English, with lancet windows in the chancel and transepts. Pevsner draws attention to the south window of the south transept, which is a five-light window with cusped intersected tracery and a quatrefoil at the top with an elongated lower lobe. The east window of the chancel is also a five-light window with intersecting tracery (Fig.108). The arcades between the nave and aisles are late thirteenth century, with quatrefoil piers. The tower is Perpendicular, with battlements and crocketed pinnacles, and the two-storeyed porch is of the same period.

Access: From Buxton take the A515 south towards Ashbourne and after about ten miles turn right into B5054 for Hartington. The church is on the right, above the market square.

(Fig 107) **St Giles, Hartington.**

(Fig 108) **St Giles, Hartington** *The interior, looking east.*

(Fig 110) **St Michael, Hathersage.**

St Michael, Hathersage

Few churches in Derbyshire, or indeed any other county, are blessed with such a superb situation as St Michael's. Like many churches with this dedication, it is high up on the edge of the community, commanding an extensive view over the Derwent valley.

The church at Hathersage apparently goes back to the twelfth century, for in 1130 the advowson for Hathersage was presented to the Priory of Launde, in Leicestershire, a priory which was said to have been founded by King Henry I with special regard for the soul of his father, William the Conqueror. No trace of a Norman church remains today, however, and St Michael's is basically a building of the fourteenth century. The arcades are supported by octagonal piers some of whose capitals are carved with a simple leaf pattern (Fig.109). Above is a clerestory, and at the west end is an excellent Perpendicular tower with a crocketed recessed spire (Fig.110).

The greatest treasures, however, are in the chancel, where there is a remarkable set of brasses of the Eyre family, who acquired the manor in the fifteenth century. In the north wall of the chancel is a very large tomb recess surmounted by an ogee-headed canopy, with brasses of Robert Eyre (died 1459) and his wife and children (Fig.111). Other brasses commemorate Ralph Eyre (died 1493) and Robert Eyre (died 1500) and their wives. Also in the chancel are an elegant set of Perpendicular sedilia (Fig.179a, p.108).

Access: Hathersage is on the A625, about nine miles west from Sheffield. On entering the village, turn right, then left steeply up Church Bank, and wind your way round the back of the church where there is a car park.

(Fig 111) **St Michael, Hathersage** *Tomb and brasses of Robert Eyre (1459).*

(Fig 109) **St Michael, Hathersage** *The interior, looking east.*

St Mary, Ilkeston

Although St Mary's has been much restored and extended in modern times, the eastern end of the church is mainly medieval and retains much interest. The manor of Ilkeston was given by William I's nephew to Robert de Muskham, and eventually it fell into the hands of the Cantelupe family; Sir Nicholas de Cantelupe is buried in the church.

From outside, the church looks Victorian, but surprises await the visitor. For the eastern half of the south arcade is clearly Norman, with circular piers, square capitals with leaf decoration, and round arches ornamented with zigzag (Fig.112). The astonishing thing about this Norman arcade is its height, and this is explained by the fact that when the tall fourteenth-century north arcade was built, the Norman arcade had to be heightened to accommodate changing taste. So the corresponding piers of the Decorated north

(Fig 113) **St Mary, Ilkeston** *Decorated arcade, with multi-shafted piers.*

arcade are octagonal with simply moulded capitals supporting pointed arches. The western halves of the nave arcades are modern.

The next surprise is the stone screen separating nave from chancel (Fig.112). Stone screens are rare, and this is one of the best. It dates from the fourteenth century, is light and graceful, and adorned with ogee arches in each division, surmounted by quatrefoils.

The chancel is separated from a north chancel chapel by a Decorated arcade with fine multi-shafted piers and arches (Fig.113). In the chancel is the effigy of Sir Nicholas de Cantelupe (died 1272), and in the south wall of the chancel there are sedilia and piscina (Fig.176a, p.107).

Access: Ilkeston is on the eastern border of Derbyshire, overlooking the Erewash valley. From Derby, take the A608 north-east towards Heanor, and after six miles turn right into A609 for Ilkeston. St Mary's is in the town centre.

(Fig 112) **St Mary, Ilkeston** *Tall Norman arcade and fourteenth-century stone screen.*

All Saints, Kedleston

Few families in England can rival the record of the Curzons for long association with one manor — for the Curzons have been in Kedleston for nearly 900 years: the present Viscount Scarsdale, Sir Francis John Nathaniel Curzon, is the thirtieth Lord of Kedleston. The manor of Kedleston was held at the time of the Domesday Survey by Gulbertus, under Henry de Ferrers, but it soon passed to Giraline de Curzon, who came to England with William the Conqueror and by the reign of Henry I (1100-1135) his son Richard was possessed of four manors — Croxall, Edinghall, Twyford

and Kedleston. Robert de Curzon, son of Richard, inherited the first three, while the younger son Thomas became possessed of Kedleston (Cox).

The Curzons held their estates originally in fee of the Ferrers, and after the disgrace of this family, to the Earldom of Lancaster, and later direct to the Crown. The advowson of the church has been held by the Curzons uninterruptedly from the beginning of the fourteenth century — the only example in the county. The church is adjacent to Kedleston Hall (described by Pevsner as the most splendid Georgian house in Derbyshire), and is thus remote from the village. Unfortunately, it is no longer used for public worship, and is now cared for by the National Trust on behalf of the Redundant Churches Fund.

Remarkably, for what was originally a village church, Kedleston has a crossing tower, with nave, chancel and transepts (Fig.114). There is a Norman south doorway, with a deformed tympanum, but apart from this the church is essentially late thirteenth century, with three-light pointed windows in the chancel and transepts. The piers supporting the central tower and the priest's door in the south wall of the chancel are also of this period.

But the attraction of Kedleston church rests not so much on its architecture, which, truth to tell, is not so remarkable, but on the internal furnishings and monuments. There is a fine set of box-pews in the chancel, dating from about 1700, and an outstanding alabaster tomb of Sir John Curzon and his wife (*c.*1450) in the south transept (Fig.115). Memorials to other Curzons of course abound: the most striking being in the north aisle added by Bodley just before the first World War in memory of the wife of Lord Curzon, Viceroy of India.

Access: Kedleston Hall is now owned by the National Trust. From the end of March to the end of October, the house is open Saturdays to Wednesdays 1pm to 5.30pm, and the grounds from 11am to 6pm. From Derby, proceed along the A6 towards Belper, but at Duffield turn left (B5023) and after half a mile left again for Kedleston.

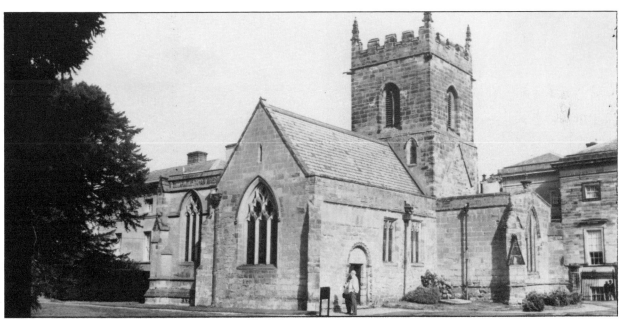

(Fig 114) **All Saints, Kedleston.**

(Fig 115) **All Saints, Kedleston** *Alabaster tomb of Sir John and Lady Curzon (1450).*

Holy Trinity, Kirk Ireton

'Ireton' means the homestead of the Irish, but it is a mystery why this name came to be applied to this village in Derbyshire. The church (or kirk) was originally a chapelry of Wirksworth, and was therefore granted along with the other church to the Dean and Chapter of Lincoln. Later it became a separate rectory.

The church is of Norman origins, as shown by the cylindrical piers supporting semicircular arches (Fig.116). The south arcade is late Norman, with simple leaf decoration beneath the capitals; the north arcade is a little later, the capitals being moulded. The west tower and south doorway are also Norman (Fig.117).

The chancel arch is Decorated, and the south wall of the chancel is occupied by one large

(Fig 119) **Holy Trinity, Kirk Ireton** *Fourteenth-century doorway in the chancel.*

(Fig 116) **Holy Trinity, Kirk Ireton** *Norman arcade.*

(Fig 117) **Holy Trinity, Kirk Ireton.**

Perpendicular arch (Fig.118) which must have been constructed when the south aisle was extended to form a south chancel chapel. There is a fine fourteenth-century doorway in the north wall of the chancel opening into a vestry (Fig.119). Cox describes this as 'an architectural gem', and remarks that the four-leaf flowers within the moulding of the arch have been cut with a precision and skill rarely encountered in parish churches.

Access: The village is most attractive, and the church is situated at the bottom of the main street on the left-hand side. From Ashbourne, take the A517 towards Belper. After about 3½ miles, turn left along a lane leading after a further 3 miles to the village.

(Fig 118) **Holy Trinity, Kirk Ireton** *Perpendicular arch (left).*

St Michael, Kirk Langley

Kirk Langley is another example of a long-lasting association between church, village and family, for the Meynells have been here for nearly 900 years. At the time of Domesday Book (1086), the manor was held by Warner, from Richard Peveril, but early in the next century it was divided into two halves — Kirk Langley, which contained the parish church — and Meynell Langley which took its name from a family of French descent, with the name variously spelt as Meignell or Mesnil. The Meynells still live in Meynell Langley, a mile away from Kirk Langley, and St Michael's contains many reminders of their rather tortuous history which is described in some detail by Cox (1879).

The church is esentially a building of the early fourteenth century, when the Early English style was giving way to Decorated. As a result, the windows of the north aisle are mainly of two lights, with simple intersecting tracery, while the east window of the chancel has four lights, with a quatrefoil in the apex (Fig.120). Those of the south aisle date from the Victorian restoration of 1885. In the south wall of the chancel is a set of early fourteenth-century sedilia with trefoiled heads and clustered shafts, and an adjoining piscina (Fig.177c, p.107). Opposite is an aumbry. There are two ancient screens of note: the tower screen, and the parclose screen at the east end of the north aisle. At the east end of the south aisle is a tomb-chest surmounted by an incised slab commemorating Henry Pole and his wife (1559).

Access: Kirk Langley is on the Ashbourne Road (A52) five miles north-west from Derby. Proceeding from Derby, St Michael's is a short distance along a lane on the left side of the main road.

(Fig 120) **St Michael, Kirk Langley** *The interior looking east.*

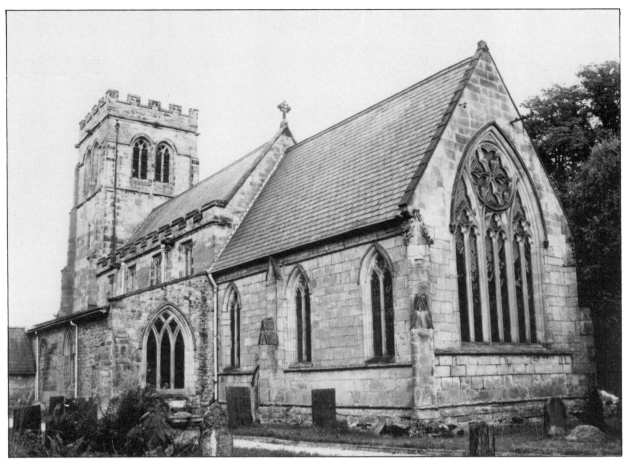

(Fig 120a) **St Chad, Longford.**

St Chad, Longford

Longford church (Fig.120a) is pleasantly
situated close to Longford Hall, a little
distance from the village. This is very
much a rural area, south of the Peak District,
and north and west of the industrial area around
Derby and in the Trent valley.

The early history of St Chad's is obscure;
Longford is not included in Domesday Book,
but Bubedene is; and Cox conjectured that the
mention of a church at Bubedene may refer to
the part of Longford parish known today as
Bupton. At any rate Longford church certainly
goes back to Norman times, as proved by the
contrasting arcades (Fig.121). The north is fine,
with round, substantial piers surmounted by
square, scalloped capitals, supporting
semicircular arches, probably dating from the
mid-twelfth century. The arch nearest the
chancel is, however, pointed and must therefore
be later. The piers and capitals of the south
arcade are originally Norman, the piers having
apparently been clumsily cut down in the
fourteenth century to support a pointed arcade
of this time. Judging by the windows, the north
and south aisles were built around 1300
(just as Early English was making way

for Decorated); the windows are of two lancet
lights with a pierced spandrel, and at the east
end of the south aisle is a three-light window
with intersecting tracery (Fig.120a). To the same
period belong the chancel arch and the chancel,
with north and south windows consisting of
two lights with early Decorated tracery. The
Perpendicular fifteenth century contributed the
fine tower, with a very tall tower arch opening
into the nave, and also a clerestory. The east
window of the chancel is Victorian.

St Chad's has an interesting array of
monuments, some of which were restored and
placed in their present position in the north aisle
in 1983-85. The effigies consist of various
members of the Longford family from the
fourteenth to the seventeenth centuries. In a
canopied recess in the south aisle is the effigy
of Sir Nicholas de Longford wearing the SS collar
(died 1402; Fig. 122). In a recess in the north
wall of the chancel is a damaged unnamed effigy,
and above are Victorian memorials to Thomas
Coke, earl of Leicester, and Anne, Countess of
Leicester (died 1842 and 1844 respectively). In
the south wall of the chancel are fine, Decorated
piscina and sedilia (Fig.177b, p.107).

Access: From Ashbourne, take the A52

(Fig 121) **St Chad, Longford** *The contrasting arcades.*

(Fig 122) **St Chad, Longford** *Effigy of Sir Nicholas Longford (1402).*

towards Derby, and after about six miles turn right along a winding road through Ednaston and Hollington. Before entering Longford village, turn right through the lodge gates towards the hall, and St Chad's is about 600 yards on the left.

St Matthew, Morley

Morley, just four miles north-east of Derby, is one of the most interesting churches in the county, and is attractively situated away from the village. The church is not mentioned in Domesday Book, the manor at that time forming part of the large estates of Henry de Ferrers. To an exceptional degree, the history of the church is closely bound with the history of the lords of the manor as revealed by the extensive series of monuments in the church.

In the twelfth century, the south arcade of two bays was built, with the semicircular arches supported by circular piers and scalloped capitals (Fig.123). The north arcade is a little later, perhaps around 1200, for the piers are still circular, the arches still rounded, but the capitals are moulded. At some time in the late twelfth century, it appears that the advowson was given to the Abbot of St Werburgh, Chester, who held it until the Reformation. The manor itself was held by the de Morley family, and during the early fourteenth century the chancel with its fine Decorated chancel arch and the south porch were added (Fig.124). Later in that century, the manor passed by marriage into the hands of Ralph Stathum. A brass in the floor of the north chapel states that Ralph Stathum had this chapel built, and died on 13 June, 1380, and that his wife Godytha, who rebuilt the present church and tower, died on 16 May 1418. So the aisles were added in the Perpendicular style, as also was the clerestory and the south chancel chapel (Fig.123) and the west tower with recessed spire (Fig.125).

The Stathums held the manor until the death of Henry Stathum in 1480, and are commemorated in the church by two brasses and a tomb-chest. The estate then again passed by marriage to John Sacheverell, who was killed in 1485 at the Battle of Bosworth Field. The Sacheverells held the estate until the eighteenth

century and there are a number of monuments of members of this family in the church. The finest undoubtedly is to Katherine who married Thomas Babington of Dethick (q.v.); she was the grandmother of the Antony Babington who was executed in 1586. Katherine Babington died in 1543, and her monument is in the north chapel.

Also in the north chapel is the best medieval stained glass in Derbyshire (Fig.183, p.109). This was brought to Morley after the Dissolution of Dale Abbey in 1538, and occupies the two easternmost windows in the north wall, with one panel containing the figure of St Ursula in the east window of this chapel. The more westerly of these two north windows contains scenes from the legend of Robert, a hermit of Knaresborough, in a series of seven compartments, and the window to the right of this shows the legend of the Holy Cross in ten compartments. The rest of the glass is Victorian. Also in the north chapel, note the many medieval encaustic floor tiles.

After the Reformation, the Sacheverells persisted as recusants for a time, and Cox writes that Mass continued to be celebrated in the north chancel chapel by priests concealed in the adjacent manor-house. But by the time of the restoration of Charles II in 1660, Jonathas Sacheverell conformed in the hope of succeeding to the estates; if so, it did him no good, for the manor passed to another branch of the family untainted with recusancy. After the Sacheverells, the Sitwells succeeded to the estates.

Access: From Derby take the A608 north-eastwards towards Heanor; St Matthew's is a short distance along a lane on the right of the main road. The church is usually locked, but the key may be obtained at the Post Office in Morley Smithy, half a mile away to the north.

(Fig 123) **St Matthew, Morley** *Norman arcade and Perpendicular arch.*

(Fig 124) **St Matthew, Morley** *The porch.*

(Fig 125) **St Matthew, Morley** *Perpendicular tower with recessed spire.*

All Saints, Mugginton

The village church of Mugginton, set on a knoll overlooking the valley of Mercaston Brook (Fig.126), is the proud possessor of an antique yew in the churchyard, so old that it is almost hollow.

The earliest part of the church is the west wall of the nave, which contains a deeply splayed window above the tower arch (Fig.127). Many authorities, including Pevsner, believe this may well be eleventh century, and Saxon rather than Norman. The lower part of the tower is Norman, and the Norman corbel-table can be seen above the window in the north side of the tower. The tower arch opening into the nave is Transitional, with a pointed arch supported by keeled semicircular responds; this combination dates it to the end of the twelfth century, as the Norman style is giving way to Early English.

The south doorway and south arcade are Decorated (early fourteenth century), and the excellent church guide points out that the capitals become slightly more complex towards the eastern end. The south aisle contains some good Jacobean box-pews. In the fifteenth

(Fig 126) **All Saints, Mugginton.**

(Fig 127) **All Saints, Mugginton** *The deeply splayed window above the Transitional tower arch is Saxon or early Norman.*

(Fig 128) **All Saints, Mugginton** *Fifteenth-century parclose screen.*

century, a Perpendicular south chancel chapel was added; this was probably erected by Nicholas Kniveton as a chantry chapel and contains the celebrated tomb-chest with its brasses of Nicholas Kniveton and his wife, dated about 1475. The chapel is separated from the south aisle by a fifteenth-century screen (Fig.128). The windows in the south aisle and in the north wall of the nave were inserted late in the fifteenth century.

Access: From Derby, take the A52 north-westwards towards Ashbourne. At Kirk Langley, turn right, and shortly afterwards fork left. Follow this lane north, and the third lane on the right leads to Mugginton.

St Mary and St Barlok, Norbury

Every county seems to have at least one odd dedication: thus Cheshire has St Bertoline (at Barthomley), Shropshire St Eata (at Atcham), and here Derbyshire has St Barlok. Apparently he was a little-known Irish abbot and bishop, but the connection, if any, between St Barlok and Norbury remains quite obscure. He appears in the window in the south-east chapel.

The church stands next to the ancient manor-house, a grouping which is very pleasing and typically English. Norbury after the Norman Conquest was part of the holding of Henry de Ferrers, but in 1076 he gave the church to the priory of Tutbury at its foundation. In 1125 the prior of Tutbury gave Norbury to William

Fitzherbert; this family held the advowson until the Reformation and the manor house until 1881; they are still lords of the manor, but the National Trust has owned the house since 1987.

The church is famous for the loveliness of its chancel, and for its monuments. The chancel is, in fact, the oldest part of the building, having been erected in the Decorated style in the first half of the fourteenth century. It is spacious and wide, and almost as long as the nave (Fig.129). The windows are so extensive that the walls between them are reduced to a minimum, anticipating the Perpendicular era. The tracery is beautiful, with complex trefoil

(Fig 130) **St Mary and St Barlok, Norbury** *Tomb of Nicholas Fitzherbert (1483).*

(Fig 131) **St Mary and St Barlok, Norbury** *Tomb of Sir Ralph and Lady Fitzherbert (1493).*

(Fig 129) **St Mary and St Barlok, Norbury** *The screen and chancel.*

(Fig 132) **St Mary and St Barlok, Norbury** *Perpendicular windows on either side of the porch contrast with the Decorated windows of the chancel.*

and quatrefoil patterns (Fig.49, p.36). There is a substantial amount of medieval stained glass, mostly of heraldic arms in grisaille. There are two very fine alabaster tombs in the chancel, commemorating Nicholas Fitzherbert (died 1473; Fig.130) and his son and daughter-in-law Sir Ralph and Lady Fitzherbert (died 1483; Fig.131). Between the tombs is the brass of Sir Anthony Fitzherbert (died 1538) and his wife. Note also the alabaster slab with the incised effigy of Alice Fitzherbert (died *c.*1460).

The nave and north aisle were built later in the fourteenth century in the Perpendicular manner. The piers are octagonal and above is a clerestory and an excellent low-pitched collar-braced roof (Fig.174, p.106). Most unusually, the south aisle really consists of two chapels, south-east and south-west, embracing the tower and porch. The windows of these chapels are Perpendicular, contrasting with the Decorated windows of the chancel (Fig.132). The oldest objects in the church are in the nave: two well-preserved Saxon cross-shafts with interlacing and an elegant Early English font.

Access: Norbury is set in lovely countryside in the Dove valley south of Ashbourne. From Ashbourne, take the A515 south towards Lichfield, and after about 4 miles turn right on to the B5033 for Norbury.

(Fig 133) **St Andrew, Radburne.**

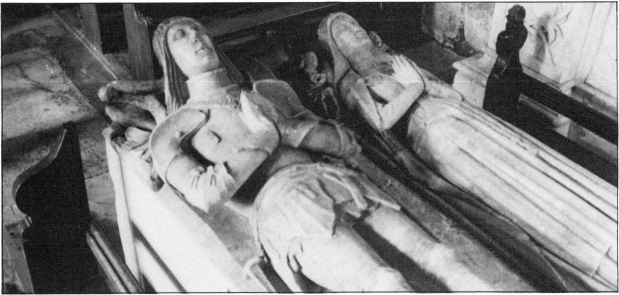

(Fig 134) **St Andrew, Radburne** *Effigies of John de la Pole and his wife (1491).*

St Andrew, Radburne

St Andrew's has a lovely situation by a stream on the edge of the grounds of Radburne Hall (Fig.133). The church consists of a nave and north aisle, separated by an early fourteenth-century arcade, with a chancel and a Perpendicular north-west tower. The early Decorated south window of the nave is especially attractive. At the west end of the church is a comfortably empanelled squire's pew. In the chancel is an unusually early pair of sedilia, the seats surmounted by Early English arches still with Norman decoration (Fig. 175b, p.107).

There are some good monuments: the best is the alabaster tomb-chest and effigies of John de la Pole and his wife, dated 1491 (Fig.134). In the north aisle stands a wall monument by Grinling Gibbons to German Pole, dated 1683. There are also two incised fifteenth-century alabaster slabs to other members of the Pole family.

Access: From Derby, take the A52 towards Ashbourne; at Kirk Langley, turn sharp left into B5020, then take the second turning right and the first left for Radburne. The church is hidden behind the former rectory, along a lane to the left and then to the right.

St Giles, Sandiacre

Sandiacre is in the extreme east of Derbyshire, between the M1 and the Erewash valley; although it is not in a particularly beautiful location, there is pleasant countryside to the west and the church is well worth visiting for the extremely high quality of its architecture. A Saxon predecessor building was mentioned in the Domesday Book, but the present edifice is clearly of Norman foundation.

The church consists simply of Norman nave and chancel arch, Early English west tower, and the splendid Decorated chancel. Cox describes the Norman work as follows: 'The inner door of the south porch is a fine Norman one, with three orders of shafts and good cylindrical mouldings. On each side of the nave is a large round-headed Norman window, with shafts and billet mouldings. The chancel arch is also Norman, of very rich character, with three orders of shafts and cylindrical mouldings (Fig.135). The shafts are clustered with a large general abacus, which is enriched with pellet and other ornaments (Fig.136). In the angles are grotesque figures. The lower part of the masonry of the tower, especially on the north side, seems also to be of Norman date; the tower of that period being taken down, almost to the foundations, to be rebuilt in the thirteenth century. The Norman work of this church is rather late in the style, *circa* 1160'.

But fine as is the Norman work, it is almost eclipsed by the splendours of the chancel, built around the middle of the fourteenth century by Roger de Norbury, Prebendary of Sandiacre 1342-47 and Bishop of Lichfield 1322-59. Externally the chancel has a moulded parapet pierced with quatrefoils and carved buttresses crowned with crocketed pinnacles (Fig.52, p.37). Three windows in the north and south walls of the chancel, and the great east window of six lights all exhibit beautiful and varied Decorated tracery; the result internally is that the chancel, spacious and dignified, is flooded with light. On either side of the priest's door in the south side of the chancel are carved heads said to be those of the reigning king (Edward III) and Queen Philippa. Also in the south wall of the chancel is an exceptionally fine set of three sedilia and adjacent piscina, all surmounted by ogee arches and crocketed canopies (Fig.178b, p.108). There is one further Decorated window inserted into the south wall of the nave. The fourteenth-century font at the west end of the nave is also very fine.

Access: From exit 25 of the M1, proceed along a small road to the north-west which leads after a short distance to the B5010 from Risley to Sandiacre. Turn right towards Sandiacre, and in the centre of the town turn left northwards. St Giles is just outside the town, on a knoll overlooking the Erewash valley. The key to the church may be obtained from the Rectory next door.

(Fig 136) **St Giles, Sandiacre** *Abacus and capital of the north chancel arch.*

(Fig 135) **St Giles, Sandiacre** *The chancel arch and chancel.*

All Saints, Sawley

Sawley is a place of great antiquity, evidently of much greater importance in previous ages than it is now. It used to be known as Sallow (willow), and the earliest reference to it is in 822 when the then Bishop of Lichfield first appointed prebendaries in his cathedral, one of which was styled Prebendary of Sawley (Cox). By the time of the Domesday Survey, the manor of Sawley was in the hands of the Bishop of Chester, and it contained two churches (those of Sawley and Wilne).

The church thus occupies an ancient site, close to the river Trent, where there was in earlier times a ferry. The oldest part of the church is the Norman chancel arch (Fig.137), and at one time it was thought that the extensive wall above was of Saxon origin. The nave and aisles were built in the Early English style by Ralph de Chaddesden (Rector, 1259-66). The piers are octagonal, the capitals simply moulded. There are lancet windows in the north wall of the nave and also in the chancel. The best window in Sawley is the east window of the chancel, which has outstanding arched tracery of the Decorated era. The windows in the south aisle are also of this time.

In the fifteenth century, the roof of the nave was raised, leaving space for clerestory windows, and the pitch was flattened providing a panelled oak roof with bosses. At the same time was built the west tower, with battlements and a recessed spire.

There are a number of interesting monuments. On the south side of the chancel is a chantry chapel endowed by John Bothe, rector of Sawley 1474-95; he was probably responsible for the fifteenth-century alterations to the church. Other Bothe monuments are in the north wall of the chancel. Then, outside the church in the south wall of the chancel, is a recess with the effigy of Cardinal John de Gauselinus, rector of Sawley 1318-46, and builder of the chancel. He was a great pluralist, being also Cardinal of St Marcelin and St Peter, Prebendary of York, rector of Hackney, and various other livings (Cox).

Access: From Derby, take the A6005 towards Long Eaton. In Draycott, just after the turning to Wilne, fork right along a road that passes close to a reservoir. This road then crosses the M1 and ends at a T-junction in Sawley; turn right, and the church is just on the left.

(Fig 137) **All Saints, Sawley** *The interior, looking east.*

(Fig 138) **St John the Baptist, Staveley.**

St John the Baptist, Staveley

The parish church gives a sorely needed dignity to Staveley, an otherwise undistinguished industrial village on the outskirts of Chesterfield. The main points of interest are the thirteenth-century west tower, and the seventeenth-century Frecheville chapel.

The tower is a prominent landmark, and is Early English, with a west door and lancet window. The upper stages are Perpendicular, the battlements and pinnacles seventeenth century (Fig.138). Inside, note the contrast between the Perpendicular south aisle, and the Victorian north aisle. In the north aisle is an ogee-headed recess which previously came from the north wall of the nave.

The Frechevilles were a powerful local family who acquired a third part of the estate by marriage in the reign of Edward I (1272-1309); another third fell into their hands in 1325, but they had to wait two hundred years for the remainder. In the seventeenth century, Sir John Frecheville was a loyal supporter of the king during the Civil War, and at the Restoration he was created a peer; he sold the estate and the advowson of the church to the Cavendishes and died, the last of his line, in 1682.

The Frecheville chapel (the south chancel chapel; Fig.139) was built by Lord Frecheville around 1676 (an unusual date for church-building), and has seventeenth-century Perpendicular windows with fine stained glass

(Fig 139) **St John the Baptist, Staveley** *The Frecheville chapel.*

of the period. The choicest is the window above Lord Frecheville's tomb, described by Pevsner as 'a splendid window of heraldic display, big, fat, scrolly foliage and cherubs'! Also in the chapel is a large monument to Christian Frecheville who died in childbirth in 1653.

Access: Staveley is on the A619, about four miles north-east of Chesterfield. The parish church is in the village centre, a short distance to the left of the main road, coming from Chesterfield.

(Fig 140) **St Mary, Tissington.**

St Mary, Tissington

Tissington is one of the prettiest and best-loved villages in the county, and is famed for its well-dressing which takes place each year on Ascension Day. The settlement is certainly very ancient, for Celtic and Anglo-Saxon burial sites were found nearby in the nineteenth century. The name Tissington is said to mean Tidsige's homestead. Domesday Book records that Tissington was among the many possessions of Henry de Ferrers, and later the estate passed to the Savage family. The FitzHerberts, who still occupy the hall, acquired the manor in the sixteenth century.

The church is basically Norman, but there were significant additions in the eighteenth and nineteenth centuries. The building occupies a prominent position in the village, situated on a small knoll not far from the hall (Fig.140). The tower is clearly Norman, with walls four feet thick at the base, and heavily buttressed at a later date. Inside the relatively modern south porch is a Norman doorway bearing a carved tympanum (Fig.19, p.23). Similar carvings are to be seen on the Norman font (Fig.181, p.108). The chancel arch is Norman, with zigzag decoration (Fig.141). The arcade to the north aisle, of Norman style, was built only in 1854. Unfortunately hiding the north side of the

chancel arch is the large, fine monument to Francis FitzHerbert (died 1619) and his son Sir John FitzHerbert (died 1643) and their respective wives. Above the chancel arch is the Royal Arms, and on the right a double-decker pulpit. Further FitzHerbert monuments are in the chancel, which was apparently rebuilt in the eighteenth century. Note the fine altar rails which are said to be late Elizabethan.

Access: From Ashbourne, proceed north on A515 for 3½ miles, then turn right through the lodge gates for Tissington.

(Fig 141) **St Mary, Tissington** *Chancel arch, FitzHerbert memorial, Royal Arms and two-decker pulpit.*

(Fig 142) **St Andrew, Twyford.**

St Andrew, Twyford

'Twyford' means 'double ford', or perhaps two fords, and the church of St Andrew is a little-known gem at the end of a lane which leads only to the river Trent. It was built only 200 yards from the river, and now has just a couple of farms for company.

Although of ancient origin, it has never become a parish in its own right, being always subordinate to Barrow-upon-Trent. From the outside it is a pretty picture, with an Early English tower, a Decorated chancel, and a brick-built ivy-clad Georgian nave (Fig.142): but appearances are partly deceptive, as the visitor will discover when he steps inside.

The interior of the church is peaceful and serene. The oldest part of the church is in fact the chancel arch, which is clearly a Norman rounded arch edged with chevron decoration. Most of the tower is indeed Early English; a pointed tower arch opens into the west end of the nave (Fig.143), and there are three lancet windows. The upper stage of the tower is later, being constructed in the early fourteenth century. The chancel also dates from this time and therefore has Decorated east and south windows. Internally the nave is of stone, not

(Fig 143) **St Andrew, Twyford** *Norman chancel arch and Early English tower arch.*

brick, and it is clear that in the eighteenth century the stonework of the nave was simply encased in brick.

Access: From Derby, take the A514 south to Swarkestone, and then proceed along the A5132 towards Willington; Twyford is on the left, about 2½ miles from Swarkestone.

St Mary, Weston-upon-Trent

St Mary's is a good example of a typical Derbyshire church, unspoilt, and set away from the village among fields near the river. Although two churches are mentioned in the manor of Westune in Domesday Book (these will be the churches of Weston and Aston), the eleventh century church at Weston has disappeared without trace, although Saxon work is still visible at Aston. The manor was granted by William I to the Earl of Chester, and later the advowson of Weston was given to St Werburgh's Abbey, Chester.

Both Cox and Pevsner draw attention to the remarkable height of the piers which separate the nave from the aisles. These are tall circular columns with moulded capitals in the Early English style, and they give a sense of height to the building unusual in a village church (Fig.144). The chancel is also Early English, with lancet windows on each side. The south aisle is probably a little later, with grouped lancets; the east window of this aisle shows the beginnings of Decorated tracery, with a circle above the lower middle lancet. The north aisle windows are clearly Decorated, with ogee tracery. The west tower is fourteenth century below, with Decorated windows at ground floor and belfry level; above are Perpendicular battlements and a recessed spire. A timber-framed south porch was added in the

(Fig 144) **St Mary, Weston-upon-Trent** *Unusually tall Early English arcades.*

seventeenth century, and according to Cox, was lucky to be spared by the Victorian restorers. Also from the seventeenth century, note the Jacobean pulpit, and the monument to Richard Sale (died 1615) with kneeling figures and a skull and cross-bones (Fig.145).

Access: From Derby, follow the A514 south, and just before Swarkestone turn left; after two miles a lane on the right (before entering Weston village) leads to the church.

(Fig 145) **St Mary, Weston-upon-Trent** *Monument to Richard Sale (1615).*

(Fig 146) **St Lawrence, Whitwell.**

St Lawrence, Whitwell

Whitwell (meaning 'white spring or stream') church is mentioned in Domesday Book, and this probably refers to a Saxon predecessor building which apparently served both Barlborough and Whitwell. The present church clearly goes back to the twelfth century, for much of the building is of Norman origin.

The west tower is Norman, and exhibits a fine doorway with one order of colonnettes, leaf capitals, and zigzag decoration in the arch (Fig.146). The external walls of both nave and chancel are Norman, and the original corbel-table can be traced all the way round under the eaves. Inside, the nave is separated from the aisles by Norman arcades, supported by thick circular piers with plain capitals (Fig.147); above is a Norman clerestory — a very unusual finding in a parish church. Notice the deep internal splaying of the clerestory windows. The chancel arch is Norman, the columns showing keeling, the capitals being scalloped with waterleaf decoration — Pevsner comments that the arch 'is clearly on the way towards Early English'.

In the fourteenth century the chancel was reconstructed and the north and south transepts added in the Decorated style. In the north wall of the chancel is an opening above which is a steep crocketed gable; this is probably an Easter sepulchre. Opposite, the sedilia and piscina are fashioned similarly (Fig.178a, p.108). In the north transept is an ogee-canopied recess (Fig.148), and in the west wall the large seventeenth-century monument to Sir Roger Manners.

Access: From Chesterfield, follow A619 towards Worksop; three miles after crossing the M1, the turning to Whitwell leaves on the right. St Lawrence's church is at the entrance to the village, on the left.

(Fig 147) **St Lawrence, Whitwell** *Norman arcades, chancel arch and clerestory.*

(Fig 148) **St Lawrence, Whitwell** *Ogee-canopied recess.*

St Chad, Wilne

St Chad was the first bishop of Lichfield (669) and he died three years later. The dedication of the church at Wilne is clearly very ancient, because it is known that as early as 822 one of the prebendaries in Lichfield held the Prebendary of Sawley and Wilne. These two churches were mentioned in Domesday Book as being held by the bishop of Chester (whither the see of Lichfield had been temporarily transferred in 1072).

With such a long lineage, it is perhaps not surprising that this remote little church should house one of Derbyshire's oldest treasures, the Saxon font (Fig.180, p.108).

This is believed to have been hollowed out of the shaft of a circular cross, and features interlaced knitwork, carvings of dragons and birds, etc.

Today, the church at Wilne stands quite isolated by the river Derwent, not far from its confluence with the Trent, the village having retreated to drier ground in Draycott. So St Chad's stands peaceably among meadows, quite bypassed by the traffic of the modern age (Fig.149). The lower part of the tower is Early English, and the arcade separating the nave and south aisle is probably also of this period — although much restored after a disastrous fire in 1917. The windows of the north side of the nave are Decorated (Fig.150), while the vaulted

(Fig 149) **St Chad, Wilne.**

south porch and the clerestory are Perpendicular. In the early seventeenth century, the south aisle was extended eastwards to form the Willoughby Chapel; this contains some excellent Flemish stained glass, and the large alabaster wall-monument to Sir John Willoughby (died 1605).

Access: From Derby, take the A6005 towards Long Eaton; in the centre of Draycott, turn right down a lane which meanders for over a mile towards the river, and the church is on the left.

(Fig 150) **St Chad, Wilne** *Decorated windows and Perpendicular clerestory.*

All Saints, Wingerworth

Wingerworth is included in this book solely because of the unusual and highly successful marriage of the architecture of the twelfth and twentieth centuries.

The Norman work is plain, probably early in the twelfth century, and consists of a south doorway, a three-bay north arcade, with circular piers, square capitals and semicircular arches, and to the right a very simple chancel arch. Above this arch is a most attractive rood-loft, the only one in Derbyshire, decorated with ribs and bosses (Fig.151). There is a medieval wall-painting on the inner face of the chancel arch. Inside the chancel (now the Lady Chapel) are Early English lancet windows. The west tower, battlements and clerestory are Perpendicular.

With the post-war expansion of the village, this small church became inadequate for the needs of the growing population, and an ambitious extension of the medieval building was erected in 1963-64. As a result, the previous nave is now a vestibule, and the new nave is entered through the Norman north arcade. The interior is constructed with pre-cast concrete

(Fig 151) **All Saints, Wingerworth** *Ancient . . .*

(Fig 152) **All Saints, Wingerworth** *. . .and Modern.*

arches (Fig.152), and there is a semicircular apse and long mullioned windows with abstract glazing (Pevsner). The contrast between the ancient and modern styles is an effective affirmation of the constancy of the Christian faith, unchanging in all generations.

Access: Wingerworth is about three miles south of Chesterfield. Proceed along the A61 through Birdholme, and the turning to the village is a fork to the right leading uphill. After nearly half a mile, the road turns sharply right, and All Saints will be seen on the left.

St Mary the Virgin, Wirksworth

If Bakewell is the archetypal Derbyshire market town, surely the much-less-visited Wirksworth must be the analogous industrial town. Although it is industrial, it is most attractively situated at the head of the valley of the Ecclesbourne and has a number of fine seventeenth- and eighteenth-century houses. Its crowning glory is, of course, the parish church of St Mary, which has many treasures to offer, especially the Saxon Wirksworth stone (Fig.12, p.17).

But Wirksworth goes back even further, to Roman times, when opencast mining of lead began to furnish the Romans with pipes, cisterns, roofs, etc. When, some centuries later, the Anglo-Saxons arrived, rights over these mines were granted to the premier religious foundation of Mercia, the abbey of Repton, founded *c*.660. When Guthlac, a monk originally from Repton, died in 714, a lead coffin was sent from Wirksworth to Crowland, Lincolnshire where another Benedictine Abbey (of St Mary, St Bartholomew and St Guthlac) was founded by King Aethelbald around Guthlac's cell.

So Wirksworth was clearly of great importance in Saxon times, and the finding of the Saxon stone confirms this. In Domesday Book, the place was still prosperous: it had a priest and a church, three carucates of land,

27 families, and three lead mines. But significant though Wirksworth church clearly was in Saxon and Norman times, there is nothing in the structure of the present building which dates from this era. Early in the twelfth century, the church was given by the King (Henry I) to the Dean and Chapter of Lincoln Cathedral; the first vicar of Wirksworth was not appointed until 1272.

From this time forward was built the present church, though much has been altered in later centuries. St Mary's is built on an impressive scale (Fig.153), with a crossing tower, transepts, and nave and chancel 152 feet long; it is notable that there is greater length to the east of the crossing tower than to the west. The massive piers supporting the crossing tower and the arcades separating the nave from the aisles are thirteenth century (Fig.154), as are the Early English lancet windows in the north and south walls of the chancel, and in the north transept; the east window of the chancel and the west window in the nave are nineteenth century.

In addition to the incomparable Wirksworth stone in the north wall of the nave, there are a number of other impressive furnishings. In both the north and south transepts are some Norman fragments which came to light during the restoration of 1870-74. The font, also in the north transept, is of late Norman origin. Amongst the collection of monuments should

(Fig 153) **St Mary, Wirksworth.**

(Fig 154) **St Mary, Wirksworth** *Early English crossing and south arcade.*

(Fig 155) **St Mary, Wirksworth** *Brass of Thomas Blackwell and his wife (1525).*

(Fig 156) **St Mary, Wirksworth** *Effigy of Anthony Gell (1583).*

be noted the brass to Thomas Blackwell and his wife (1525; Fig.155), the monument to Antony Lowe (died 1555; Fig.168, p.103), the incised alabaster slab to Ralph Gell (died 1564) and the tomb-chest and alabaster effigy of Anthony Gell (died 1583; Fig.156).

Access: Wirksworth is about six miles south of Matlock. Proceed along the A6 towards Derby, and at Cromford the B5036 leads to Wirksworth. The church is in the centre of the small town, hidden behind some shops on the left.

(Fig 157) **All Saints, Youlgreave.**

All Saints, Youlgreave

Tourists flock in season to see the justly famous well-dressing at Youlgreave, but the all-the-year-round attraction of the village should rightly be the parish church, one of Derbyshire's finest; and the church guide, by John and Mary Bartlett, gives an excellent account of the building.

Youlgreave is certainly an ancient settlement, being mentioned in Domesday Book as having

(Fig 158) **All Saints, Youlgreave** *Tomb-chest and small alabaster effigy of Thomas Cokayne (1488).*

(Fig 159) **All Saints, Youlgreave** *Alabaster panel commemorating Robert and Joan Gilbert and their family.*

a mill, but no church. The name is variously interpreted as meaning 'auldgroove — old mine', or 'yellow grove' — such is the uncertainty which often surrounds old English place-names!

The present church dates from Norman times — i.e. the twelfth century — but there may well have been a Saxon predecessor building which has vanished without trace. The arcades are Norman, and it is interesting to compare the two: the south is late Norman (*c.*1160), with circular piers, square capitals with scallop decoration below, and round arches (Fig.13, p.19); the north is later still (1180-1200), with circular piers and Norman capitals, but the arches are pointed (i.e. Transitional; Fig.33, p.28). The south aisle windows are late Early English: they show simple Y-tracery, indicating a date around 1300 — on the verge of the Decorated era. The Perpendicular age (fifteenth century) contributed the western extension of the nave, the impressive west tower, with angle buttresses, battlements and pinnacles (Fig.157); late Perpendicular are the clerestory and the low-pitched, panelled roof of the nave with carved bosses at the intersections of the timbers.

Some of the artefacts in the church are extraordinarily good. In the north wall of the nave is a fine carving of a figure carrying a staff and pouch, thought to represent a pilgrim. The Norman font near the south door is remarkable for the presence of a projecting side stoup; apparently it originally belonged to the daughter chapel at Elton, and in the early nineteenth century was a bone of contention between the two parishes. In the chancel is a fourteenth-century effigy of a knight holding a heart in his hands. Also in the chancel is the tomb-chest of Thomas Cokayne (died 1488); since he died while his father was still alive, his fine alabaster effigy is small (Fig.158). But the finest monument of all is the alabaster panel commemorating the family of Robert Gilbert (died 1492; Fig.159). This is now a reredos behind the altar in the north aisle and depicts the Virgin and Child, flanked by Robert and Joan Gilbert and their seventeen children, seven boys behind their father, and ten girls behind their mother. Its original place is thought to have been behind an altar in a chantry chapel at the east end of the south aisle.

Access: From Bakewell, follow the A6 southwards towards Matlock, and just past Haddon Hall turn right on the B5056, and then after a further mile, right again to Youlgreave. The church is on the left in the centre of the village.

The Age Of Religious Strife — 1550-1700

The age of religious strife did not leave Derbyshire unscathed. Although the Elizabethan religious settlement was generally accepted in London and the south-east, elsewhere in the country the old faith was maintained for a while with varying degrees of success; and in Derbyshire in particular Catholicism retained the allegiance of a substantial proportion of the aristocracy. After the papal excommunication of Elizabeth in 1570 (which declared her Catholic subjects free of allegiance to her), tension heightened and the persecution of Catholics was intensified. Some of the old Derbyshire families were noted recusants: the Eyres of Hathersage, Fitzherberts of Norbury, Sacheverels of Morley, Foljambes of Chesterfield, Babingtons of Dethick among others (Childs). There is no doubt that the presence of Mary Queen of Scots in the neighbourhood acted as a magnet and focus of allegiance to a number of the local gentry; after the discovery of the Babington plot and the execution of the Queen, priests hidden in Catholic houses were hunted down and three were executed in Derby in 1588. Many of the old aristocracy suffered for their faith, none more than the Fitzherberts of Norbury: Sir Thomas Fitzherbert after thirty years of confinement in various places died in the Tower of London in 1591.

After the Reformation, church building in Derbyshire, as elsewhere in England, came virtually to a halt, and, with rare exceptions, during the next 150 years was limited to repair work and essential maintenance. The Civil War was fought in Derbyshire, but without the destruction of parish churches that occurred, for example, in Cheshire and Shropshire. The only new churches of this period are at Risley (1593), Carsington (1648) and Foremark (1662), and all are built in the Perpendicular style — a case of Gothic Survival — rather than in the new style being developed in London and elsewhere by Inigo Jones and his successors. Seventeenth-century chapels were built at Staveley and Wilne, and interior furnishings of this period are well preserved in a number of Derbyshire churches, particularly Castleton, Dale Abbey, Foremark, Kedleston, and Mugginton.

St Saviour, Foremark

Foremark means 'old fort' and from 1271 the church there was known to be a chapel under the care of Repton. By the mid-seventeenth century, this chapel, and that of nearby Ingleby, were ruinous, and the present

(Fig 160) St Saviour, Foremark.

building was erected in 1662 by Sir Francis Burdett to serve both communities.

The style is entirely Perpendicular and only the expert can differentiate it from the true Perpendicular of 1350-1550. To increase the verisimilitude, stones from Ingleby chapel were used in building the bell-tower, and also the churchyard walls, of St Saviour's. The west tower and the nave are embattled in the best Perpendicular manner, and there are two five-light Perpendicular windows placed symmetrically in the north and south walls (Fig.160).

Internally, the church is a delight, with its seventeenth-century furnishings intact (Fig.161). There is a complete set of box-pews and on each side of the nave Burdett funeral hatchments and the Royal Arms. Towering above the congregation is a superb three-decker pulpit: the lowest level was reserved for the clerk who led the worshippers' responses; from the intermediate level, the priest conducted the service; and he then ascended to the top level to deliver the lengthy sermon. Above the top deck, a sounding board provided the necessary resonance.

The chancel is separated from the nave by a graceful rood- screen with plain glass in the central section and stained glass above. The wrought-iron communion rails are the workmanship of Robert Bakewell, who also constructed the chancel screen in Derby Cathedral.

Access: St Saviour's is not an easy church to find! From Repton, take a road eastwards towards Milton. At the beginning of this village, fork left, and after half a mile an unmarked track on the right leads to St Saviour's. At the entrance, a notice says 'Repton Preparatory School HGV vehicles only'. Proceed along this track, and the church is 400 yards on the left.

(Fig 161) **St Saviour, Foremark** *Seventeenth-century interior.*

The Eighteenth Century

A cynic might say that the age of religious strife was followed by the age of apathy. Certainly, once the Protestant Succession was secured by the Glorious Revolution of 1688, the heat was taken out of the religious issue, and a new era of Englightenment began, bringing with it an increasing degree of toleration. In some areas the Church of England became somewhat somnolent, till roused by one of its more turbulent priests, John Wesley. In Derbyshire by the eighteenth century the Catholic issue at last subsided; by now the great majority of the leading families were Protestant, and the discord of the previous 150 years was a thing of the past.

Church building of a mostly undistinguished quality occurred, and new churches were built in such villages as Mapleton (Fig.162), Trusley and Stoney Middleton. But there was only one church of the first rank built in the county during this century, and that was All Saints, Derby, with which this survey of Derbyshire churches concludes.

(Fig 162) **St Mary, Mapleton.**

St Martin, Stoney Middleton

St Martin's is unusual because of the octagonal shape of its eighteenth-century nave. A warm spring was known here near the site of the present church in Roman times, and in the medieval era was dedicated to St Martin. It is probable that a well-chapel was built here, like the ancient chapel of St Anne at Buxton.

In 1415, a church was built here by Joan Eyre in thanksgiving for the safe return of her husband Robert from the Battle of Agincourt. This church would have been under the care of the mother church at Hathersage, where many members of the Eyre family are interred. Of Joan Eyre's church, only the Perpendicular west tower remains (Fig.163), and by the eighteenth century the rest of the building had become ruinous.

So in 1759 the present remarkable octagonal nave was built to the design of an architect who, according to Cox, but not to Pevsner, also designed the stables at the back of the Crescent in Buxton, the stables at Chatsworth, the rectory at Eyam, and Stoke Hall. Cox comments acidly that 'We cannot help wishing that he had confined his attention exclusively to secular work'. But although it would, perhaps, be difficult to describe the nave as beautiful, it is undoubtedly impressive, and nicely decorated

(Fig 163) **St Martin, Stoney Middleton.**

inside. There is an ambulatory with circular windows, and a lantern storey supported by piers.

Access: Stoney Middleton is on the Baslow to Castleton road, A623, 2½ miles north-west from Baslow. The church is on the right.

All Saints, Derby (Derby Cathedral)

It appears that the city of Derby was founded by King Edward *c.*925 following the reconquest of the area from the Danes. There was an earlier Saxon settlement covering a much wider area called Northworthy; this had a minster church, St Alkmund's by at latest 800 — a collegiate foundation with a staff of six canons. St Alkmund was a son of the Northumbrian King Alhred and he was buried here *c.*802, the church being dedicated to him (Craven). Earlier still the Romans had a fort known as Little Chester on the opposite bank of the river Derwent. By the time of Edward the Confessor (1042-66), Derby had at least eight churches: St Alkmund's and All Saints (both collegiate foundations); the others were St Mary's, St Peter's, St Michael's, St Werburgh's, St Helen's and St James's. St Helen's became absorbed in Darley Abbey, the most important monastic house in the county, and the church

of St James was given to the Cluniac monks at Bermondsey who established a priory. St Mary's disappeared in the Middle Ages without trace, but the others survived.

St Alkmund's became a place of pilgrimage because the relics of the saint were removed from Lilleshall, Shropshire, where he died, to Derby. The medieval church of St Alkmund was pulled down in 1841, and a new building erected on the site. This in turn was demolished in 1967 to make way for the inner ring road. From the old St Alkmund's, a fragmentary Saxon cross-shaft and a superb Anglo-Saxon sarcophagus may be seen in the Derby Museums and Art Gallery.

The churches of SS Michael, Peter and Werburgh remain; some Norman work survives in St Peter's, but the others have been totally rebuilt, St Michael's in 1858 and St Werburgh's in 1699 (the chancel) and 1892-94; unfortunately, St Werburgh's is no longer used for worship.

All Saint's, too, has had a troublous history. Like St Alkmund, it was founded as a collegiate church with a dean and six prebendaries, around 943, apparently by the King, Edmund. This was the time when Derby had been recaptured by the Anglo-Saxons from the Danes. Early in the twelfth century, the church, with Wirksworth, was given by King Henry I

(Fig 164) **All Saints, Derby** *Perpendicular tower.*

(Fig 165) **All Saints, Derby** *Georgian nave, wrought iron chancel screen, and twentieth-century retro-choir.*

to the Dean and Chapter of Lincoln Cathedral. Of the medieval church, little is known and nothing survives. There must have been a west tower, and presumably this became unsound for it was pulled down and the present magnificent Perpendicular tower was built between 1510 and 1530. In 1549, during the reign of Edward VI, the college was dissolved, but papal supremacy was restored during the reign of Mary I (1553-58). In 1556, Joan Waste, aged 22, who was poor and blind, was burned as a heretic because she refused to accept the doctrine of transubstantiation.

By the early eighteenth century, the condition of the body of the church had become so bad that the building was demolished and the present church was built to the design of James Gibbs in 1725. Gibbs was a Scot, a friend and pupil of Sir Christoper Wren, and a Roman Catholic; because of his faith he was dismissed as a commissioner for building new churches in London in 1715. In the capital, his best-known works are St Mary-le-Strand, the tower of St Clement Danes, and the church of St Martin-in-the-Fields. He was one of the most influential eighteenth-century architects, and his 'Book of Architecture' published in 1728 was widely acclaimed both in England and in America (Randall). In 1745, the Young Pretender, bonnie Prince Charlie, attended a

service in Gibbs' church, and it was in Derby that he made the fateful decision to call off his march to London (where King George II was hastily packing his bags in preparation for flight) and to return to Scotland where he was defeated at Culloden.

From earliest times, Derby and its shire had been in the diocese of Lichfield, but in 1884 Derbyshire and most of Nottinghamshire (which had been in the diocese of Lincoln) were transferred to the new diocese of Southwell. Then, in 1927, the diocese of Derby was created, and the parish church of All Saints became the new cathedral. Finally, in 1967-72, the eastern extension of the cathedral was built, to the design of Sebastian Comper. All Saints' thus has three major components — the sixteenth-century tower, the eighteenth-century nave and the twentieth-century chancel.

The tower (Fig.164) is one of the finest Perpendicular towers anywhere in the country. It is said to be the second highest tower in England built for a parish church (212 feet). With its great height, it dominates the city of Derby. It has three storeys, each decorated with friezes. Above the clock are blank three-light Perpendicular windows, with much decoration. The bell-openings are tall, and again in the Perpendicular manner. At the top are battlements and pinnacles. The angle buttresses

(Fig 166) **All Saints, Derby** *View of the east end from across the River Derwent.*

are decorated with crockets and pinnacles, giving the whole tower an appearance of sumptuous prosperity. It appears that much of the cost of the tower was raised by 'church ales' held in various places in the county; these were local feasts, at which entertainment such as morris-dancing, cudgel-playing, shooting at the butts and other sports were provided to raise money for various good causes.

The interior of All Saints' is a feast of colour and delight (Fig.165). Try to visit on a sunny day, when the light streams through the large windows in the south wall of the nave, bringing out the subtle yellows, blues and greens of the modern stained glass windows on either side of the chancel. These are by Ceri Richards, and represent (on the north) All Souls and (on the south) All Saints. The nave is separated from the aisles by Tuscan columns with Doric capitals from which spring the groin-vaulting of the aisles and the tunnel-vaulting of the nave. The sense of light and spaciousness is profound. At the west end is a gallery, from which an excellent view of the interior may be obtained.

The showpiece of the church is the wrought-iron screen which spreads across both nave and aisles. It was designed by Gibbs and is the work of the Derby smith Robert Bakewell (1682-1752). The delicacy of the design has been likened to lacework, and the screen separates nave and chancel without obstructing the view. Above the central gates are the Royal Arms of George II, including the fleur-de-lys of France (these were still the days when the sovereigns of England claimed also to be sovereigns of France — a legacy from the Hundred Years' War of Edward III). In the north side of the chancel stands the bishop's throne, of Greek Orthodox origin from Constantinople; the upper part is believed to be from an icon-stand of the sixteenth century, the seat being added in the seventeenth. Note also the two civic pews in the front of the centre aisles; on the south side is the Mayor's pew decorated with Bakewell ironwork, and on the north the County Council pew with modern ironwork designed by the Cathedral architect, Anthony New.

Beyond the screen is the modern chancel, designed by Comper (Fig.166). Above the High Altar is a canopy with a triangular pediment and Corinthian columns. The chancel harmonises perfectly with the eighteenth-century nave and has clearly brought the whole concept of the new cathedral to a fitting conclusion.

In the south aisle are steps which lead down to St Katharine's chapel, now set aside for private prayer. It was formed from the outer chamber of the Cavendish family vault. There are a number of monuments in the cathedral, notably those to Caroline, Countess of Bessborough, William Ponsonby, Earl of Bessborough, and of course Bess of Hardwick, Countess of Shrewsbury. An hilarious account of the famous Bess by the Reverend Henry Thorold is contained in the guide to Derby Cathedral, by James Landsberger, on sale in the cathedral shop.

Works of Art in Derbyshire Churches

Alabaster monuments

The county is famous for alabaster, the material which was so widely used in churches for a period of three hundred years from about 1350 onwards. Alabaster is a compact marble-like form of gypsum (calcium sulphate), and was quarried at Chellaston, a few miles south of Derby, and at Tutbury, just over the border in Staffordshire. So it is not surprising that the centre of the industry was here in Derbyshire and in Nottingham, whence alabaster was sent all over the country, and also to the continent. Gardner, who systematically studied the subject, points out that alabaster is soft, easy to work, and is well-suited for taking colour and gilding. He also established that only Yorkshire (34), a much larger county, had more alabaster monuments than Derbyshire (29).

The earliest alabaster monument in Derbyshire is the unique half-length wall-monument to Sir Godfrey and Lady Foljambe in Bakewell, dated 1385 (Fig.76, p.49). Mural tablets of this sort later became common, but none other is known of this period.

A century later (1492), the Gilbert monument at Youlgreave (Fig.159, p.92) is also of a most unusual form; originally this was probably a reredos panel of a chantry chapel altar. Also at Youlgreave is the diminutive tomb-chest and effigy of Thomas Cokayne (Fig.158, p.92). The finest assemblies of effigies are at Ashbourne, Chesterfield and Norbury. Others are at Ashover, Bolsover, Longford, Morley, Sudbury (Fig.167), Tideswell and Wirksworth (Fig.168). The shrouded effigies at Fenny Bentley are well known. Even more gruesome, perhaps, is the monument to William, first Earl of Devonshire and Henry Cavendish at Edensor: one appears as a skeleton, the other in his shroud with the face exposed (Fig.169).

Less costly to prepare were the incised alabaster slabs which are found occasionally, e.g. at Barlow (Fig.170) and Crich (Fig.90, p.56).

Woodwork

Derbyshire is not well known for the quality of its ecclesiastical woodwork, but there are some pleasing exceptions. The *screen* at Fenny

(Fig 167) **All Saints, Sudbury** *Monument to John and Mary Vernon (1600).*

(Fig 168) **St Mary, Wirksworth** *Chest tomb of Anthony Lowe (1555) with the Royal Arms behind.*

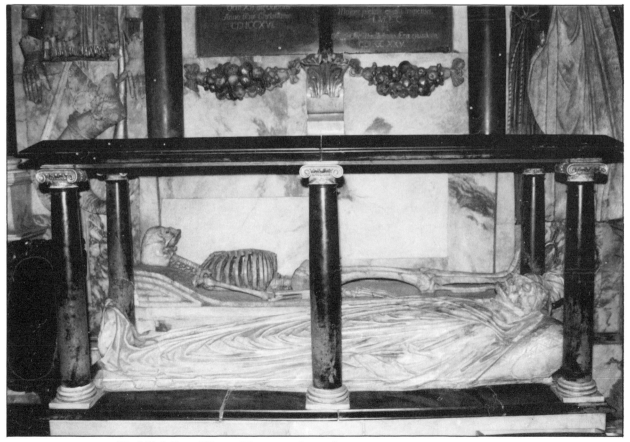

(Fig 169) **St Peter, Edensor** *The memorial to William (1625) and Henry (1616) Cavendish.*

(Fig 170) **St Laurence, Barlow** *Incised alabaster slab to Robert Barley and his wife (1467).*

(Fig 171) **All Saints, Brailsford** *Carved bench-end.*

Bentley is the finest in the county, and those at Chesterfield and Great Longstone, amongst others, are worth noting. *Box-pews* survive in several churches, including Castleton (the best), Dale Abbey, and Kedleston. The carved bench-ends at Brailsford (Fig.171) are good. A number of *pulpits* are fine, including an unusual rectangular one at Alsop-en-le-Dale (Fig.172), and Jacobean examples at Chesterfield and Dronfield (Fig.173); then there is the double-decker at Tissington and the triple-decker at Foremark. There are several fine Perpendicular *roofs* of low pitch and decorated with bosses at the intersections; the best include Great

(Fig 172) **St Michael, Alsop-en-le-Dale** *Rectangular pulpit.*

(Fig 173) **St John the Baptist, Dronfield** *Jacobean pulpit.*

(Fig 174) **St Mary and St Barlok, Norbury** *Low-pitched Perpendicular roof.*

(Fig 175) **Sedilia, (a) Monyash (b) Radburne** *late twelfth century and early thirteenth century respectively.*

(Fig 176) **Sedilia, (a) Ilkeston (b) Bakewell (c) Brailsford** *late thirteenth century.*

(Fig 177) **Sedilia, (a) Church Broughton (b) Longford (c) Kirk Langley** *early fourteenth century.*

Longtone, Norbury (Fig.174) and Repton. The best tie-beam roof is at Tideswell (Fig.63, p.42).

Sedilia and piscinae

Sedilia are seats for the clergy, usually three in number, sometimes only two, situated invariably on the south side of the chancel. Sometimes they are all on the same level; in other chancels they are at different levels, the highest nearest the altar being reserved for the most senior priest.

The piscina is the basin for washing the vessels used at Mass, provided with a drain; when found in a church it always means that an altar was placed nearby; the usual arrangement is that the piscina is in the wall to the south of the altar, and when associated with sedilia it is placed just to the east of the row of seats.

Derbyshire has a considerable number of sedilia of high quality, and a series of twelve is illustrated here (Figs.175-179) covering a period of two hundred years from the late twelfth to the late fourteenth centuries. The earliest is undoubtedly Monyash (Fig.175a), late Norman rounded arches decorated with dogtooth; a little later is Radburne (Fig.175b) now with pointed arches as the style is giving way to Early English. Later in the thirteenth century are the sedilia at Ilkeston (Fig.176a), Bakewell (Fig.176b) and Brailsford (Fig.176c); at Ilkeston and Bakewell the piscina is arched with an early ogee-shaped canopy, indicating a transitional phase from Early English to Decorated. From early in the fourteenth century come the sedilia from Church Broughton (Fig.177a), Longford (Fig.177b) and Kirk Langley (Fig.177c); these have pointed trefoil

(Fig 178) **Sedilia, (a) Whitwell (b) Sandiacre** *mid-fourteenth century.*

(Fig 179) **Sedilia, (a) Hathersage (b) Tideswell** *late fourteenth century.*

(Fig 180) **St Chad, Wilne** *Saxon font.*   (Fig 181) **St Mary, Tissington** *Norman font.*

heads. Towards the middle of the fourteenth century, at the height of the Decorated period, are the splendidly gabled and crocketed ogee-canopied specimens at Whitwell (Fig.178a) and Sandiacre (Fig.178b). More restrained are the late fourteenth-century Perpendicular sedilia at Hathersage (Fig.179a) and Tideswell (Fig.179b); these are less steeply arched, with a horizontal moulding above.

Fonts

Derbyshire is not a good county for fonts, only

(Fig 182) **St Oswald, Ashbourne** *Early English font.*

(Fig 183) **St Matthew, Morley.**

the remarkable lead font at Ashover (Fig.66, p.44) being of national importance. The oldest by far is the Saxon font at Wilne (Fig.180); this comes from part of a circular cross, and has carvings of dragons and birds. Norman fonts include Tissington (Fig.181), with crude carving of a snake and animals, Chesterfield (Fig.55, p.39), Eyam (Fig.25, p.23) and Hognaston (Fig.26, p.24), the last two showing carvings of blank arcades on columns. The best Early English font is at Ashbourne (Fig.182) with trefoil arches and fleur-de-lys between. Finer than all these is the Decorated font at Bakewell (Fig.75, p.49) showing figures under broad crocketed ogee arches.

Stained glass

The best medieval stained glass in Derbyshire comes from Dale Abbey and is now at Morley (Fig.183). At Dalbury, there is a lovely small figure of St Michael (Fig.184). Other good glass is at Ault Hucknall, Ashbourne, and Norbury. Seventeenth-century glass may be seen in the chapels at Staveley and Wilne. There is, of course, a large amount of Victorian stained glass, but this is outside the scope of this book.

Glossary

Abacus: a flat slab above a capital.

Achievement: a display of armorial bearings.

Advowson: the right of presentation of a priest to a church.

Ambulatory: an enclosed walkway.

Apse: the semicircular or rectangular end of the chancel.

Arcade: a range of arches supported by piers or columns.

Arch: curved supporting structure, made of wedge-shaped sections.

Aumbry: a recess or cupboard to hold the vessels for Mass or Communion.

Ball-flower: Ornamentation used in the Decorated period consisting of a globular flower of three petals enclosing a small ball.

Balustrade: a series of short columns, usually supporting a railing.

Bay: the space between the columns of an arcade.

Beakhead: a Norman ornamental motif, with stylised heads of birds or animals with long beaks pointing downwards, used on arches or above doorways.

Billet: a Norman ornamental motif with short raised rectangles placed at regular intervals.

Boss: a projection placed at the intersection of the ribs of a vault or roof.

Box-pew: a pew with a tall wooden enclosure.

Broach spire: a spire at the base of which are sloping half-pyramids of stone to effect the transition from a square tower to an octagonal spire.

Buttress: a mass of masonry projecting from or built against a wall to give extra strength.

Cable moulding: moulding resembling a twisted cord.

Capital: the top part of a pier or column.

Carucate: the land a team of oxen can plough in a season.

Ceilure: an embellished part of the roof above the rood-screen.

Chancel: the east end of the church in which the altar is placed.

Chancel arch: an arch at the east end of the nave opening into the chancel.

Chantry chapel: a chapel endowed for the saying of Masses for the souls of the founders after death.

Chapel of ease: a chapel for worshippers at some distance from the parish church.

Chapelry: the jurisdiction of a chapel.

Chevron: Norman zigzag moulding on arches or windows.

Clerestory: an upper storey of the walls of the nave pierced by windows to give additional light.

Collar-beam: a tie-beam applied high up the slope of a roof.

Collar-braced: Collar-beams supported by curved timbers.

Colonnade: a row of columns.

Colonnette: a small column.

Corbel: a block of stone projecting from a wall, often supporting beams of the roof from its horizontal upper surface.

Corbel-table: a series of corbels.

Corinthian columns: one of the Orders of classical architecture.

Crocket: decorative projections on the sloping sides of spires, pinnacles, etc.

Crossing: in a cruciform church, the space at the intersection of the nave, chancel and transepts.

Cupola: a domed or polygonal turret crowning a roof.

Curvilinear: see Tracery.

Cushion: in Norman architecure, the rounding-off of the lower angles of the capital to the circular pier below.

Cusp: a tooth-like ornament found in Gothic tracery.

Dado: the lower part of the screen.

Decorated: historical division of English Gothic architecture, covering the first half of the fourteenth century.

Dog-tooth: late Norman and Early English decoration consisting of a series of ornamental square pyramids.

Doom: a picture of the last Judgment.

Dormer window: an upright window projecting from a sloping roof.

Drip-stone: see Hood-mould.

Early English: historical divison of English Gothic architecture, covering the thirteenth century.

Easter sepulchre: a recess in the north wall of the chancel used to house the consecrated host between Maundy Thursday and Easter Day.

Fan vault: see Vault.

Fee: a grant of land for feudal service.

Fillet: a narrow flat band running down a shaft.

Fret: ornamental network.

Frieze: a decorated band along the top of the tower.

Gargoyle: a stone water-spout draining a gutter, often grotesquely carved.

Geometrical: see Tracery.

Gothic: the style of architecture characterised by pointed arches, sub-divided into Early English, Decorated and Perpendicular.

Greek key: a fret pattern.

Grisaille: greyish tints in stained glass.

Half-timbered: see Timber-framing.

Hammer-beam: a horizontal beam projecting from the wall, carrying arched braces and struts.

Hatchment: the arms of a deceased person placed in a lozenge-shaped frame.

Herring-bone masonry: in which the component blocks are laid diagonally, alternate courses lying in opposing directions making a zigzag pattern on the face of a wall.

Hood-mould: projecting moulding over a door or window to throw off water.

Ionic columns: one of the Orders of classical architecture.

Jamb: the straight side of an archway, doorway or window.

Keeling: moulding whose outline in section is like the keel of a ship.

Lancet window: the tall, narrow, pointed window of the Early English period.

Lantern: an open structure surmounting the crossing, with windows all round.

Light: a vertical division of a window.

Lintel: a horizontal stone over a doorway.

Long-and-short work: corner-stones placed with their long axes alternately upright and horizontal.

Misericord: a bracket on the underside of a hinged seat in the choir-stalls, providing the occupant with some support while standing.

Mullions: vertical stone bars dividing a window into 'lights'.

Nail-head: Early English ornamentation consisting of small pyramids regularly repeated.

Narthex: a vestibule at the western end of a church.

Nook-shaft: a shaft in the angle at the side of a doorway or window.

Norman architecture: the massive Romanesque style of building prevalent from 1066 to the end of the twelfth century.

Ogee arch: an arch formed by two S-shaped curves, with the concave parts above coming to a point; typical of the fourteenth century.

Order: one of the successively recessed arches of an archway; at the sides of a doorway, all the parts of a column, with base, shaft, and capital.

Parclose screen: a screen separating a chapel from the rest of the church.

Pediment: a low-pitched gable, placed as a decorative feature above doorways, windows, etc.

Perpendicular: historical division of English Gothic architecture, from c.1350-1550.

Pelta: a small shield.

Pier: a column of free-standing masonry supporting arches.

Pilaster: a shallow pier attached to a wall.

Piscina: a basin with drain on the south side of the altar for washing the vessels used during Mass.

Plate tracery: see Tracery.

Portico: a roof supported by columns at the entrance to a building.

Quatrefoil: an ornament divided by cusps into four lobes.

Recusant: a person, especially a Roman Catholic, who refused to attend the Church of England.

Recessed spire: a spire recessed within a parapet.

Reredos: an ornamental screen or hanging on the wall behind the altar.

Respond: a half-pier carrying one end of an arch and bonded into a wall.

Reticulated tracery: see Tracery.

Romanesque: an alternative name for Norman architecture, defined by round arches and vaults.

Rood: a Cross bearing the body of Jesus, flanked by the Virgin Mary and St John.

Rood-loft: a gallery on top of the rood-screen.

Rood-screen: a screen placed at the junction of the nave and chancel, in medieval times bearing the rood.

Sacristy: a room for housing sacred vessels, vestments, etc.

Saltire: an equal-limbed cross set diagonally.

Scallop: decoration on the under surface of a capital, in which a series of truncated cones are elaborated.

Sedilia: recessed seats for priests in the south wall of the chancel.

Spandrel: the space between the curve of an arch and the enclosing mouldings.

SS collar: a collar awarded to those in the service of John of Gaunt, Duke of Lancaster in the late fourteenth century.

Stiff-leaf: Early English type of foliage of many-lobed shapes.

String-course: a projecting line of moulding running horizontally round the walls of the church or tower.

Tester: a canopy over the pulpit.

Three-decker pulpit: a pulpit, with clerk's stall and reading desk below.

Tie-beam: a horizontal timber connecting the feet of the rafters.

Tower arch: an arch usually at the west end of the nave opening into the ground floor of the tower.

Tracery: intersecting ribwork in the upper part of a window.

  Curvilinear: Tracery consisting of curved lines.

  Geometrical: consisting of circles or foiled (leaf-shaped) circles.

  Plate: an early form of tracery in which openings are cut through the stone in the head of the window, often producing a Y shape.

  Reticulated: tracery in which circles are drawn at top and bottom into ogee shapes producing a net-like pattern.

Transept: transverse portion of a cross-shaped church.

Transitional: the style of building in which Gothic pointed arches exist alongside Norman architecture; typical of 1160-1200.

Transom: a horizontal bar across the opening of a window.

Trefoil: an ornament divided by cusps into three lobes.

Tuscan columns: one of the classical Orders of architecture.

Tympanum: space between the lintel of a doorway and the arch above it; sometimes applied to the space above a rood-screen.

Vault: an arched roof or ceiling.

  Fan-vault: A vault in which all the ribs springing from their origin are of the same length and curvature, and equidistant from each other.

Vine-scroll: a Saxon ornamental motif, with plants depicted in a scroll pattern.

Volute: a spiral scroll, often found on capitals.

Y-tracery: see Tracery, plate.

Zigzag: Norman geometrical decoration found on arches, etc.

Bibliography and References

The standard work on Derbyshire churches is the four volumes entitled *The Churches of Derbyshire* by J.Charles Cox, published in 1875-79. Cox goes into great detail into the parochial history and also into the genealogy of the great Derbyshire families associated with the parish churches. The work is invaluable as a source of reference, but is inevitably showing its age.

The other indispensable book is Nikolaus Pevsner's *Derbyshire* in *The Buildings of England* series, revised by Elizabeth Williamson in 1978 (Penguin Books Ltd., Harmondsworth). This gives an authoritative modern view on the churches as buildings, but is perhaps less helpful in guiding the uninitiated to those churches which are really worth visiting.

Other references:

Childs, J. (1987) *A History of Derbyshire.* Chichester.

Craven, M. (1988) *Derby: an Illustrated History.* Derby.

Ekwall, E. (1960) *The Concise Oxford Dictionary of English Place-names.* (Oxford).

Esdaile, K.A. (1946) *English Church Monuments 1510-1840.* London.

Foster, R. (1981) *Discovering English Churches.* London.

Gardner, A. (1940) *Alabaster Tombs of the Pre-Reformation Period in England.*

Gem, R. (1989) *Melbourne, Church of St Michael.* Archaeological Journal vol.146. Supplement, pp.24-30.

Hinde, I. (1985) *The Domesday Book: England's Heritage, then and now.* London.

Jones, L.E. (1978) *The Beauty of English Churches.* London.

Keyser, C.E. (1904) *A List of Norman Tympana and Lintels.* London.

Morris, R. (1989) *Churches in the Landscape.* London.

Randall, G. (1982) *The English Parish Church.* London.

Taylor, H.M. (1989) *St Wystan's Church, Repton. A Guide and History.* Derby.

Vallance, A. (1936) *English Church Screens.* London.

Wilson, D.M. (1984) *Anglo-Saxon Art.* London.

Index

Page numbers in **bold** refer to to main entries of the various churches

Adda 11
Adelulf 26
Aethelbald 11, 13, 16, 89
Aethelflaed 18
Aethelred 16
Aethelwold 26
Aidan, St 33
Alabaster 102
Alfred the Great 18
Alkmund, St 18, 97
Alsop-en-le-Dale 21, 105, 106
Ashbourne 9, **30-35**, 36, 102, 109
Ashford-in-the-water 21, 23, 53, 64
Ashover 21, **44-6**, 102, 109
Astbury 43
Aston Eyre 21
Aston-upon-Trent 10, 13, **46**
Atcham 77
Athelstan, King 18
Auden, W.H. 54
Augustine, St. 11
Ault Hucknall 21, 23, **47-8**, 109

Babington, Antony 58, 59, 74
Babington family 45, 58, 94
Babington, Katherine 74
Babington, Thomas 44-6, 74
Bakewell 9, 11, 16, 30, 31, **48-9**, 53, 64, 102, 107, 109
Bakewell, Robert 95, 101
Barlborough 87
Barlok, St 77
Barlow 103, 104
Barrow-upon-Trent 84
Barthomley 77
Beakhead 20
Beckermet St John 17
Beresford family 62, 63
Bertoline, St. 77
Bess of Hardwick 101
Bessborough, Countess of 101
Bessborough, Earl of 101
Betti 11
Billet 20
Black Death 43, 56
Blackwell 17
Blackwell, Thomas 90
Bolsover 21, 23, **49-50**, 102
Boothby family 35
Boothby, Penelope 35
Bosworth Field, battle of 74
Bothe, Rev.John 81
Bower, Sir Thurstan de 41
Box-pews 105
Bradbourne 13, 16, **51**, 53
Bradbourne family 35
Brailsford 17, **52**, 105, 107
Brampton 32
Brassington **53**
Breadsall 32, 37, 43
Breadsall Priory 20
Breaston 29, 36
Breedon-on-the-Hill 16, 17, 53
Bubedene 72
Bunbury 43
Bupton 72
Burdett, Sir Francis 94
Buxton 96

Cantelupe family 68
Canute, King 18
Carlisle 26
Carsington 94
Castleton **53-4**, 94, 105
Cavendish Chapel 49
Cavendish family 49, 101, 102
Ceadda 11, 87
Celtic church 11
Chad 11, 87
Chaddesden 37
Chaddesden, Ralph de 81
Charles Edward, Prince 99
Chartley Hall 58
Checkley 17
Chellaston 102

Chester, Abbey of St Werburgh 74, 85
Chester, Earl of 53, 85
Chesterfield 9, 21, 36, **37-9**, 102, 105, 109
Chevron 20
Church Broughton 21, **54-5**, 107
Cokayne family 35, 92, 93, 102
Comper, Sebastian 99, 101
Crich 28, **56**, 103
Crowland Abbey 89
Croxall 68
Cryer, Rev.Samuel 54
Cubley 36, **57**
Curzon family 68, 69

Dalbury 109, 110
Dale Abbey 20, **57-8**, 74, 94, 105, 109
Danegeld 18
Danelaw 18
Danes, the 11, 18
Darley Abbey 20, 97
Darley Dale 17
Decorated architecture 36, 37
Denby 43
Derby 18, 97
Derby, All Saints 9, 43, **97-101**
Derby Cathedral 9, **97-101**
Derby, St Alkmund 16, 17, 18, 43, 97
Derby, St Helen 97
Derby, St James 97
Derby, St Mary 97
Derby, St Michael 43, 97
Derby, St Peter 97
Derby, St Werburgh 18, 97
Dernall Abbey 53
Dethick 45, **58-9**
Devonshire, Countess of 47
Devonshire, Earl of 102
Diuma 11
Dog-tooth 20, 29, 30
Domesday Survey 19
Dronfield 37, 105, 106
Dunstable Priory 53

Early English architecture 30
East Bridgford 45
Eata, St 77
Eckington **59-61**
Edensor 102, 103
Edinghall 68
Edmund, King and St. 53, 97
Edward, King 18, 48
Edward the Confessor 18, 97
Edward I 53
Edward III 80
Edward VI 99
Elton 93
Elizabeth, Queen 58, 94
Ethelred, King 18
Ethelred the Unready 18
Evesham 14
Eyam 16, 21, 23, **61-2**, 109
Eyre family 67, 94, 96
Eyre, Philip 45

Fenny Bentley **62-3**, 102
Ferrers, Henry de 19, 54, 65, 68, 74, 77, 83
Findern 21
Fitzherbert families 58, 77, 78, 83, 94
Foljambe family 39, 41, 49, 94, 102
Fonts 108, 109
Foremark **94-95**, 105
Frecheville family 82

Gauselinus, Cardinal John de 81
Gell family 90
George II 99
Gibbons, Grinling 79
Gibbs, James 99
Gilbert, Robert 92, 93, 102

Gosforth 17
Great Budworth 43
Great Longstone 43, **64**, 105, 107
Gregory I, Pope 11
Guthlac 89

Harold, King 18
Harrying of the north 19
Hartington 65
Hastings, battle of 18
Hatchments 64
Hathersage **66-7**, 96, 108
Henry I 26, 67, 89, 97
Herringbone masonry 13
Hobbes, Thomas 47
Hognaston 21, 23, 24, 109
Hope 17, 40, 53
Hucknall Torkard 47
Hunt, Rev. 61
Huthwaite 47

Ilam 17
Ilkeston **68**, 107
Ingleby 94, 95
Iona 33

John, King 40, 64

Kedleston **68-9**, 94, 105
Kilpeck 24
Kirk Ireton **70-71**
Kirk Langley **71**, 107
Kniveton, Nicholas 77

Lancet windows 30
Launde Priory 67
Leek 17
Leicester, Earl of 72
Lilleshall Abbey 97
Lindisfarne 33
Little Chester 97
Long-and-short work 13, 14
Longford **72-3**, 107
Longford family 72, 102
Lowe, Antony 90, 103

Malpas 43
Manners family 49, 87
Mapleton 96
Mary I, Queen 99
Mary, Queen of Scots 58, 94
Melbourne 9, 19, 20, **24-7**
Mercia 11, 18
Meverill, Sir Sampson 41
Mompesson, Rev.William 61
Montgomery, Sir Nicholas 57
Monuments 102
Monyash 107
Morley 30, **74-5**, 102, 109
Mugginton 13, **76-7**, 94

Nailhead 20
Nantwich 43
New, Anthony 101
Newcastle, Duke of 49
Norbury 17, 36, **77-8**, 102, 106, 107, 109
Norbury, Roger de 80
Norman building 19, 20
Northumbria 33
Northworthy 97
Nostell Priory 26

Offa 11, 16
Ogee arch 36
Oswald, King and St 11, 30, 33
Oswy 11

Parwich 20, 21, 23
Peada 11
Penda 11
Perpendicular architecture 42, 43
Peveril, William de 49, 53
Pews, box 105
Philippa, Queen 80
Pilasters 13

Piscinae 107, 108
Plague, bubonic 43, 61
Pole families 56, 71, 79
Pulpits 105
Pursglove, Bishop 41

Radburne **79**, 107
Redundant Churches Fund 68
Repton 9, 11, **13-15**, 20, 30, 53, 107
Richards, Ceri 101
Risley 94
Rolleston family 45, 58
Roofs 43, 105-07
Ryknield Street 37

Sacheverell family 74, 94
Sale, Richard 85
Sandiacre 37, **80**, 108
Savage family 47, 83
Sawley **81**
Saxon building 11, 13
Saxon crosses 15-17
Scallop 19
Scarcliffe 21
Screens 102, 105
Seckington 11
Sedilia 107-108
Shrewsbury, Countess of 101
Sitwell family 61
Stanley, Rev.Thomas 61
Stanton-by-Bridge 13, 29
Stathum family 74
Staveley 82, 94, 109
Steetley 9, 19, 20, **21-5**
Stoney Middleton **96-7**
Sudbury 102

Taddington 17, 37
Taylor, Dr H.M. 11, 13-15
Thorpe 22
Tideswell 9, 36, 37, **39-41**, 43, 102, 107, 108
Tissington 21, 23, **83**, 105, 108, 109
Tong 49
Transitional building 27, 28
Tree of Life 16, 21
Trusley 96
Tutbury 54, 58, 77, 102
Two Dales 17
Twyford 68, **84**
Tympana 20, 21

Vale Royal Abbey 53
Vernon family 49, 103
Vine-scroll 16
Volute 20

Wakebridge, Sir William de 56
Walsingham, Sir Francis 58
Waste, Joan 99
Well-dressings 83, 91
Werburgh, St 18
Wesley, Rev.John 96
Weston-upon-Trent **85**
Whitwell 21, 22, 28, **86-7**, 108
Wiglaf, King 11, 13, 14
William I 18, 19
William II 33, 37
Willoughby family 88
Wilne **87-8**, 94, 108, 109
Wingerworth **88-9**
Wirksworth 9, 30, 56, **89-90**, 102, 103
Wirksworth Stone 17, 18
Woodwork 102-108
Wulfhere 11
Wystan, St 11, 14, 54

Y-tracery 30, 36
Youlgreave 9, 19, 20, 21, 28, **91-3**, 102

Zigzag 20